Note the following printing errata:

Page 62-*First line is missing:*
On the 17th, Vincent's Brigade suffered during a long march

Page 76-*First line is missing:*
Within minutes of its arrival on Little Round Top, Vincent's

Page 121-*First line is missing:*
house, simply because it was one of the structures closest to the

Pages 55, 75, 88, 97, 120-*First line repeated from previous page.*

COLONEL STRONG VINCENT.

What Death More Glorious

A Biography of

GENERAL STRONG VINCENT

By
James H. Nevins and William B. Styple

Belle Grove Publishing Co.
Kearny, N.J.
1997

ISBN 1-883926-09-2
Copyright © 1997
James H. Nevins and William B. Styple
All rights reserved.
Library of Congress Catalog Card Number: 97-93093
Belle Grove Publishing Co.
P.O. Box 483
Kearny, N.J. 07032
Printed in the United States of America.

Table of Contents

1

FOREWORD

In the late afternoon of July 2nd, 1863, on the western slope of Little Round Top, a single minie ball removed Colonel Strong Vincent from the Third Brigade of the First Division, Fifth Corps, and dispatched the young commander to the next world and to the history books. Unfortunately, his life and sacrifice received too little historical notice for too many years.

Ten years ago my wife, Myra, and I began to focus our attention on the crucial events of Little Round Top and the men who filled key roles in that most pivotal and bloody conflict. We soon found to our suprise that even in his home town of Erie, the memory of Strong Vincent's major contributions to the outcome of the Battle of Gettysburg had faded over the decades like an old battle banner.

Our admiration of Strong Vincent increased as we examined his life and studied his actions while walking the ground where he spent his last lucid hours. We learned of his early years, his work and education, his early entry and rapid rise in the military, the natural leadership he exhibited, and the deep respect in which this young citizen-soldier was held by his subordinates and superiors. Strong Vincent emerged from the mists of history and stood tall as a model for present generations.

The fate of war led Strong Vincent and his brigade toward the tumult of the south end of the Federal line that stifling and fearful afternoon. The stuff of which he was made propelled him in a new direction, to Little Round Top, to the rebel flanking movement, and to the last hours of his life.

As he brought his brigade into view of the Wheatfield, Vincent rode forward to intercept a messenger frantically trying to deliver orders to the division commander. Time was of the essence. Grasping the situation, Vincent demanded that the orders be given to him. Upon seeing the tactical importance of the stony hill to his left rear, he announced "I will take the responsibility of taking my brigade there." Without hesitation, he detached his brigade of some eleven hundred men from the divsion and raced to the undefended heights. How many men are capable of making such a judgment and taking such decisive action?

As Vincent neared the summit of Little Round Top, he hurriedly eyed the terrain and posted his four regiments in the best possible position using the slopes of the hill and the boulders and rocks to maximum advantage. His speedy and judicious deployment of his troops proved to be crucial within minutes as the onrushing rebel forces collided with his hastily formed defensive line.

Under heavy attack, the right of the brigade line began to falter and fall back towards the summit. Vincent sped to the breach and leaped onto an exposed position to rally his men forward into the line. He was an easy target. He was struck down by a single blow.

During the next few hours of heavy fighting Vincent's men remained as he had placed them. The brigade held. The gray line was stopped. The Union line remained anchored on Little Round Top.

Here for the first time, the life and deeds of that remarkable young man are presented to us and preserved for future generations by authors Jim Nevins and Bill Styple. Their efforts ensure that Strong Vincent will take his proper place in Civil War literature and will never be forgotten.

Readers, especially the younger ones, will learn of a man's devotion to his country, personal bravery, judgment, initiative and decisiveness. We are confident that more and more readers will come to admire Strong Vincent as we do. We hope that readers will be inspired to emulate Vincent by exercising individual judgment, being decisive, and at some times in their lives will be moved to declare, "I will take the responsibility myself." We hope that they too will find Strong Vincent to be a man for our times.

James R. Wright
Canfield, Ohio

PREFACE

In the course of four years of civil war, a total of 628,944 soldiers, Americans all, lost their lives.1 Included in this number are the 9,775 souls, Federal and Confederate, killed on the battlefield at Gettysburg.2   All of these men paid for their convictions with their life's blood, and each of them is entitled to the highest honor, in perpetuity, that their country can bestow. In the acknowledgment of the enormous contribution that these men -- and those fortunate enough to have survived -- made to their respective causes, it must be noted that some gave even more than their lives to the nation's great struggle. These are the men who contributed their carefully-honed competence, their skilled judgment, and their inspirational leadership in the face of the enemy.   These are the men whose unwavering spirits remain forever on the field of battle, remembered, even after 130 years, for their superb moments of glory. These are the men who gave their lives, and more.

Colonel Strong Vincent, of Erie, Pennsylvania, commanded the Third Brigade of the First Division in the Army of the Potomac's Fifth Corps at Gettysburg. His independent decision, on the second day of the three-day battle, to extend the Union left onto an undefended hill called Little Round Top, is generally acknowledged to have been a primary factor in the resistance of a Confederate flank attack.   Soon after he skillfully positioned his troops along the rocky slope and instructed them "to hold this ground at all costs,"3 the rebel forces attacked with such ferocity that a portion of Vincent's Brigade began to withdraw from the battle line in terror.   As Vincent gallantly stood on the hillcrest rallying the faltering men, he was mortally wounded, and died five days later in a Gettysburg farmhouse.   The order authorizing his promotion to brigadier general arrived only hours before his death.

When my interest in the Civil War began to focus sharply on the second day of Gettysburg, I found that most historians had limited Strong Vincent's contribution to a paragraph or two, or perhaps even to a footnote.   Only the man who served as Vincent's bugler, Oliver Norton, thought his Colonel's accomplishment worthy of a full volume.   *The Attack and Defense of Little Round Top* is primarily a collection of letters from battlefield commanders, with commentary by Norton. This work, published in 1913, was developed from a shorter version of the same theme published by Norton in 1909, which expanded on his original effort, a pamphlet printed circa 1902.

Norton's paramount focus was the role of Vincent's Brigade at Gettysburg, and his book is a credible source for a myriad of details about the second day of the battle. Elsewhere, the military exploits of the Eighty-third Pennsylvania and of Vincent's Brigade have been adequately documented, so this project will not present a detailed account of battles or a unit history.

In over 130 years, no biography has been written which commits to text the life of a man who was a decisive figure in the bloodiest battle ever fought on American soil. Consequently, our present efforts will lack the detail found in other heroic biographies whose authors had the benefit of a continuum of information.   Our disadvantage extends even to the collection of correspondence between Colonel Vincent and his wife, which vanished -- untranscribed -- in 1914.   Similarly, most of the artifacts kept by the loyal Oliver Norton were lost after his death in 1920.

Offered here are only the bits and pieces remaining in the dusty recesses of human record. It is undoubtedly impossible, at this late date, to do justice to the memory of this noble man, but it is our resolve to honor him as best we can.

J.H.N.

ACKNOWLEDGEMENTS

The assistance of a myriad of people was invaluable in the research and writing of this book.

Without the help of Myra and Jim Wright, who spent years investigating the life and times of Strong Vincent for the sheer joy of it, this book would have been virtually imposible to write. Words cannot express our profound gratitude.

We sincerely appreciate the valuable contributions of Brian Pohanka; John and Iris Sachs and family; Harry Hunter; Drs. William Kiser, F.T. Hambrecht, S. Altic, and Ira Rutkow; the Erie County Historical Society; U.S. Army Military History Institute, Carlisle Barracks; Gettysburg National Military Park; Scott Hartwig; Mike Ruane; Charles F. Johnson; Christina L. Wolfe; Harvard University Archives; Peter Hakel; Irwin Rider; Rev. B.B. Vincent Lyon, Jr.; Steve L. Zerbe; Joe Pinto; Craig Caba; Mike Kraus; Kathy Georg Harrison; Todd Meisenhelter; Evelyn Nevins; Laura Nevins; Nancy Styple; Ronn Palm; Jack Fitzpatrick; Rob Hodge; Bob Crickenberger and our fellow members of Vincent's Brigade.

J.H.N.
W.B.S.

What Death More Glorious

A Biography of
GENERAL STRONG VINCENT

Strong Vincent, circa 1849.

CHAPTER I
"Nobody can be idle about me."

The boy hated school. Now that he had reached his fourteenth birthday, he saw no reason to continue at the Erie Academy. His father -- Bethuel Boyd Vincent, who preferred to be called "B.B.", -- presumably feigning agreement in hopes of an eventual change of heart, replied, "Very well, my son, but nobody can be idle about me. If you leave school, you must go into the foundry."[1]

The foundry, conveniently enough, was owned by the boy's father, the latest endeavor in a lifetime of successful business ventures centered around the family's home in Erie, Pennsylvania. For the next six months, a young laborer named Strong Vincent sweated beside the workers in the iron foundry of Vincent, Himrod & Co.

Born June 17, 1837, he was the first child of eight -- although three of his siblings would die before their fourteenth birthdays -- of Bethuel Boyd Vincent, whose French Huguenot ancestors had arrived in America in1687, and Sarah Strong Vincent, a descendant of Massachusetts Bay Colony settlers. Perhaps in reaction to his own pretentious name, B.B. Vincent had an aversion to common names, long names, middle names, and nicknames. His offspring all bore single monosyllabic monikers: Strong (named for his mother's family), Blanche, Belle, Boyd, Rose, Kate, Reed, and Ward.2

Strong's mother had been a farm girl, and married B.B. in 1834. She was so uncommonly beautiful, family tradition maintains, that when she was a baby during the War of 1812, soldiers passing her family's farm carried her off in their arms to show her to the camp. In 1825, legend has it that the Marquis de Lafayette's attention was so drawn to the lovely thirteen year old, as she watched his entourage go by, that he dismounted from his horse to kiss the pretty little girl.3

Strong was born at the home of his paternal grandfather, Judge John Vincent, at the corner of First and Cherry Streets in Waterford, Pennsylvania. His parents' home, just around the corner at First and High Streets, was somewhat more humble than the judge's, who had made his fortune in the mercantile and freight business between Waterford and Erie. In 1843, when B.B. Vincent moved his family twelve miles to Erie, the family consisted of three children: Strong, who was six, Blanche, age four, and one-year-old Belle.

The Vincent and the Strong families were well-acquainted with each other long before the union of B.B. and Sarah. The families had been instrumental in pioneering the vicinities of Erie and Waterford, which were originally the forts of Presque Isle and LeBoeuf. Both families were successful entrepreneurs, similar in their moral philosophies, and devoted to strict Christian principles. The Strongs had built a "Union Church" on their farm for the use of all denominations. The Vincents were staunch members of St. Peter's Episcopal Church in Waterford, where six-month old Strong was baptized, and later, of St. Paul's Church in Erie.4

As an old man, Strong's younger brother, Boyd, wrote

about the religious and moral discipline of the Vincent family: "Bible-reading, family prayer, study of Sunday-school lessons, strict Sunday observance, carefully regulated amusements....Each boy had to take his share, too, of the daily 'chores' about the house, caring for the horses and cows, building fires, carrying coal and ashes and blacking all the shoes every Saturday night. 'No lazy boys about me. Don't stand back and wait for the other fellow. Jump in and put your own hand to it': these were constant injunctions. [Our father] was nearly six feet tall and weighed 225 pounds; and when he said 'Come' we came, and when he said 'Go' we went."5

As the months wore on at the foundry, young Strong rose to the occasion. True to his name, he developed a remarkable physical strength, persevering in the arduous occupation of iron moulder. He was also an uncommonly bright lad, and Mr. Vincent undoubtedly soon realized that his son's efforts would be more valuable in the areas of administration and management. His father transferred him to the counting-room, where Strong eventually was given charge of the books, and was overseeing much of the labor force in the foundry. But by the age of seventeen he again found himself discontented with the ordinary course of events. He now thought he could best serve his family's business interests by acquiring a formal technical education -- a lofty ambition for a boy who had quit school at the age of fourteen.

Strong left home to enter the Scientific School at Trinity College, Hartford, Connecticut, in 1854. Although the institution still exists, Strong's academic records have not survived. He was probably an average student, and joined a social and literary club called "The Order of the Black Book."6

Soon after entering Trinity, Strong was described by a friend as "a young man of excellent principles and studious habits, who bids fair to justify the high expectations of his immediate friends and relatives."7

Bethuel Boyd Vincent

Sarah Ann Vincent

After two years at Trinity, Strong entered Harvard University, and his motivation for doing so remains the source of some controversy. Various sources seem to be in general agreement with an essay by William Willard Swan, one of the few 19th century biographical sketches of Vincent, which was published in *Harvard Memorial Biographies* in 1866. Swan says that Vincent was not content at Trinity: "The reputation of Harvard had a charm for him.... He had been so hurried in his first fitting for college, that he deemed it better to lose a year, rather than enter the class corresponding to his class at Trinity, and therefore entered as sophomore in the Class of 1859."[8]

Trinity alumnus Charles F. Johnson provides a different insight into Strong's reasons for transferring to Harvard. As a Trinity undergraduate in 1940, Mr. Johnson attended a lecture by Judge Philip McCook (1873-1963), son of Dr. John McCook (1843-1927), a Trinity contemporary of Strong Vincent. Judge McCook, hoping to inspire young students with tales of honor and gallantry, related his father's story that Vincent was expelled from Trinity. He explained that Vincent, in his sophomore year, went calling on Miss Elizabeth Carter, a teacher at Miss Porter's school in Farmington, ten miles west of Hartford. At some point, a guard or watchman voiced a comment that impugned the lady's virtue, and, as Johnson so aptly phrases it, Vincent "responded to the affront with the same gallantry and vigor he was later to display in the Civil War." McCook's account indicated that the man was repeatedly pummeled, which effectively rendered him unconscious.[9]

Additional credence is given to this account from an exchange of letters which repose in Trinity College's archives, discovered there by Mr. Johnson. These letters seem to refer to the incident, and the propriety of publicizing it. The first, dated December 17, 1912, is from Edgar Waterman, Trinity College Treasurer, to Dr. Edward M. Gallaudet, LL.D., the college

President:

> Your account the other evening down at the Chapter House as to why General Strong Vincent, who was for some time a member of the class of 1858, left College and the events leading up to it, was very interesting. If at your leisure you would send me a written narrative of this event we would appreciate it very much and it would make a valuable part of the biographical material which we already have concerning General Vincent.

Dr. Gallaudet, Trinity class of 1856 and therefore a contemporary of Vincent's, sent this terse reply to Waterman the following day:

> Replying to yours of yesterday, I must say that I do not think it would be wise to make public the story I told of Strong Vincent's escapade at Farmington & its consequences.
> Certainly not in the lifetime of Mrs. Vincent.
> I do not think Gen. Vincent would wish to have the matter brought up at this late day.
> I had no idea, when telling the story that anyone would wish to have it made public.10

In light of the event that precipitated his departure from Trinity, it is not known how Vincent managed his way into Harvard. Of course, it is possible that his father's wealth may have made his Harvard welcome more cordial, but, certainly, his appearance and demeanor were considerable factors. Swan says: "Vincent was a man of mark in his Class and in the College. There was not a student, from Senior to Sophmore, who did not on first meeting him seek to learn who he was. Physically he seemed fully developed. Of rather above medium height, he had a well-formed and powerful frame, and his face was remarkably striking and handsome. He looked many years older than he really was, and in every respect his mind corresponded to his body. One would have said, on hearing him converse, that he was twenty-five years old. "

And yet, Swan continues, Vincent "was not a hard student. If the old recitation list were to be consulted, the marks against Vincent's name would hardly predict a life of such credit to himself and his College. "11

Vincent's academic and diciplinary records at Harvard are difficult to interpret by today's standards. Generally, his grades were quite poor in his first (sophomore) year but steadily improved until his senior year, where he made a good scholastic showing. Students were graded for recitations, which were oral examinations to see if students had learned their lessons. These marks were tallied for each semester and their aggregate gave class rank.   Strong Vincent's senior year, fall semester, aggregate was 12427 placing him 46th out of a class of 92. For the spring semester his aggregate was 15873 placing him 51st in his class. Vincent occasionally received private admonishments for "missing prayers" and "smoking in the yard. " Although such misconduct appears to have been quite typical at 19th century Harvard, it should be noted that Vincent, in his senior year, led his class in absences from prayers, with a total of fourteen violations.12

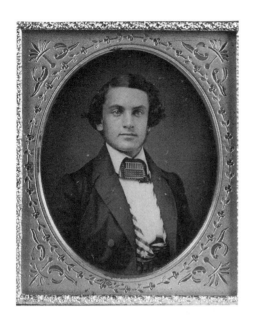

Strong Vincent circa 1854.

Strong Vincent circa 1855.

Strong Vincent, Harvard Class of 1859.

CHAPTER II
"I thought him a dude
and an upstart."

Vincent graduated from Harvard in June of 1859, returned to Erie, and began to study law in the office of William S. Lane, a leading lawyer of the county. Within two years he had been admitted to the Bar and had become Lane's partner. He occupied a prominent business position and was influential in the public affairs of the city and county. Strong Vincent stood high in the estimation of his fellow-citizens.

Vincent took great interest in the political campaign of 1860, supporting the candidacy of Abraham Lincoln. After the election, when war seemed a virtual certainty, militia companies began forming throughout the North. Following the rebel attack on Fort Sumter and Lincoln's call for volunteers, Vincent enlisted, as a private, on April 14, 1861, in the Wayne Guards, a three-month regiment being raised in Erie by Mexican War

veteran Colonel John W. McLane.   On the following day,
Vincent was commissioned Second-Lieutenant of Company A.1

Ever since his days at Trinity, Vincent kept up his romance
with the woman whose honor he defended in 1856 -- Elizabeth
Carter, described by a friend as "a tall, handsome, clever girl,
dark-haired and dark-eyed."   After his enlistment, Strong
quickly telegraphed Elizabeth, still a teacher at Miss Porter's
School, to tell her of his determination to take up the sword. He
also mentioned he thought it would be best for her to become his
wife immediately, before he went off to war.   She consented,
and they were married in the Reformed Dutch Church in Jersey
City, New Jersey, on April 25, 1861. Unwilling to be separated,
the bride then accompanied her husband to Pittsburgh, where the
Wayne Guards had been ordered.

The *Erie Weekly Gazette* reported of Vincent, "Our young
friend having prevoiusly enlisted, is now 'off to the wars' as
Adjutant of the Regiment from his District.   We trust he may
safely return to his fair bride after filling the demands of his
country upon his services, and thereafter enjoy long continued
and uninterrupted domestic felicity."2

Vincent was promoted to First Lieutenant and Adjutant of
the regiment on May 1st.   Oliver Willcox Norton, a private in
the Eighty-third, wrote many years after the war of his initial
impression of Strong Vincent:

> My first recollection of him is his appearance as
> adjutant in forming the line of the regiment for its dress
> parade. As I stood, a private in the ranks, and heard his
> command on the right, "To the rear in open order,
> March!" and saw the line officers step to the front in an
> irregular line and heard him correct their faults, then saw
> him march to the center, halt, turn on his heel, face the
> colonel, who stood like a statue at some distance with his

arms folded, gauntlets reaching near his elbows, salute with his sword and report, "Sir, the parade is formed." I confess my first impression of him was not favorable. I thought him a dude and an upstart. I soon came to know that he wished to impress on that mob of green country boys, by example as well as precept, the proper way for a soldier to stand and move. It was the beginning for that regiment of its military education.3

Camp Wilkins, in Pittsburgh, was made the rendezvous for all volunteers from the western part of Pennsylvania, and Colonel McLane was appointed commander of the camp. Lieutenant Vincent, as McLane's adjutant, was kept busy in the organization of the regiment and in the training of the volunteers.

The Wayne Guards never left Pittsburgh, and shortly before the Union defeat at the battle of Bull Run, the ninety-day volunteers were discharged. Vincent believed his services still belonged to his country, and began taking an active part in raising, with Colonel McLane, a three-year regiment--the Eighty-third Pennsylvania Regiment of Volunteers. For his tireless efforts, Vincent was appointed Major. The Eighty-third Pennsylvania was mustered into United States service on September 8th with men from Erie, Crawford, Warren, Venango, and Mercer counties represented in the ranks.4

Second Lieutenant Strong Vincent in April 1861.

Elizabeth "Lizzie" Carter Vincent.

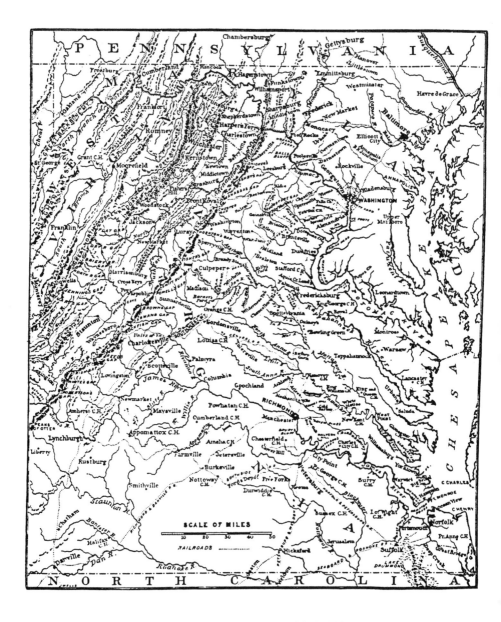

Virginia during the Civil War

CHAPTER III
"Surely the right will prevail."

Just after leaving for the war, Major Vincent wrote to his wife: "Surely the right will prevail. If I live, we will rejoice over our country's success. If I fall, remember you have given your husband to a sacrifice to the most righteous cause that ever widowed a woman."[1]

Elizabeth knew the risks of military service, but she encouraged Vincent to do his full duty. "It was not military glory," wrote a friend who knew the couple, "but the purest patriotism which actuated both."[2]

Major Vincent was sent to Washington ahead of the Eighty-third to procure weapons, tents, blankets, and other equipage. The regiment reached Washington on September 20, 1861, and was first quartered at Meridian Hill, Maryland, where the men were armed with antiquated smoothbore Harper's Ferry muskets.[3]

While there, an election was held by the Eighty-third to determine field officers. Strong Vincent was voted Lieutenant Colonel and Louis Naghel of Indiana, Pa., Major. One week later the Eighty-third relocated to Hall's Hill, Virginia and traded their inferior smoothbore weapons for the preferred Springfield rifled musket. The regiment was assigned to Brigadier General Daniel Butterfield's Third Brigade of Major General Fitz John Porter's Division. A man of Vincent's ability did not long escape the notice of his superiors and he was frequently called away on other duties, being employed much of the winter as brigade inspector.

One day in November a new regiment, the Forty-fourth New York, was assigned to the brigade. Colonel McLane called his officers together and suggested the new regiment share the hospitality of the Eighty-third. As the new arrivals halted and stacked arms, McLane, Lieutenant Colonel Vincent, and the staff of the Eighty-third approached the officers of the Forty-fourth New York and invited them to share their supper. A close friendship soon developed between the two regiments.4

These regiments were forever after to be known as "Butterfield's Twins." A veteran later wrote: "A generous rivalry sprang up, each regiment striving to outdo the other in drill, discipline, and all the manifold duties of a soldier's life. Although under different officers, the two organizations were like one great regiment."5

By now the Third Brigade was composed of the Eighty-third Pennsylvania, Seventeenth New York (replaced later by the Twelfth New York), Forty-fourth New York and the Sixteenth Michigan.

A soldier in the Eighty-third wrote: " We now commenced the work of soldiering in good earnest." Colonel McLane taught his men the school of the soldier and soon his regiment was considered one of the best in the army. An officers' school was also established to study maneuvers and tactics, and Lieutenant Colonel Vincent became the schoolmaster. "He made a good one," remembered one veteran, "what he did not know about tactics and army regulations he learned, and forced the junior officers to learn and practice."6

With the lives of his men depending on him, Vincent's diligence had to make up for his lack of formal military training. One soldier wrote of Vincent's dedication: "Without the schooling of West Point, by the help of his trained mind, quickness of perception, and constant study, stimulated by his intense patriotism, his knowledge of the art of war made him equal to any emergency in which he was placed."7

The men in the ranks began to admire Vincent's soldierly conduct and devotion to duty. One enlisted man of the Eighty-third remembered: "Vincent was of medium stature, but well formed. He was a fine horseman, and when mounted looked much larger than when on foot. He was a gentleman by nature, quiet and considerate in his demeanor, deserving and receiving the respect of his men and officers, as well as that of his superiors in rank. Severe in discipline when severity was needed, no officer in the army was more thoughtful and considerate of the comfort and health of his men."8

The Eighty-third became so noted for their proficiency at drill as to become the subject of a commendatory order from General Butterfield: "The General commanding feels called upon to congratulate and commend the Eighty-Third for the very general spirit of attention to duty that seems to pervade the regiment. Their attention to drill is especially recommended as a worthy example to the rest of the brigade."9

For this skill, the Eighty-third Pennsylvania was awarded a distinctive uniform: a complete French foot chasseur outfit, ordered from Paris by the U.S. Quartermaster General. The honor was mitigated, however, when a great many of the French-made uniforms proved too small for the Pennsylvanians. The chasseur uniforms were worn until March 1862, when the regiment was ordered to take the field. The men packed up their French uniforms and placed them in storage, and there is no indication they were ever worn again.10

During the winter of 1861-1862, Elizabeth Vincent traveled to Virginia and for a few weeks lived with Strong in camp.   "I am most thankful that she had those weeks in the camp," wrote her close friend, Sarah Porter, "They were comparatively quiet, and she thoroughly enjoyed them.   I have less fear than I had before her marriage of her tranquil happiness, and I am very glad that she feels that Erie is her home."11

The Eighty-third Pennsylvania held a ceremony on Washington's birthday, 1862. A private wrote home: "Today is a great day in the army, the cannons roar & the bands are playing. We were called out today formed in a hollow square four deep facing inwards where were the Colonel and staff, chaplain, & the adjutant and band. While we gave our attention at parade rest, Lt. Col. Vincent read George Washington's farewell address to us after which the band played several nationall [*sic*] airs and the chaplain closed with a very appropriate prayer."12

In March 1862, the Eighty-third was included in a reconnaissance mission near Fairfax Court House, Virginia, to determine if any of General Joseph Johnston's Confederates remained in the Manassas area. Finding no enemy there, the Eighty-third was recalled to Alexandria to join the rest of the Army of the Potomac on Major General George "Little Mac" McClellan's Peninsular Campaign. McClellan's plan was to side-step the rebel army in his front, and capture the Confederate capital of Richmond from the southeast. From the beginning, the men believed this would be the campaign that would end the war. A private in the Eighty-third wrote home: "I hope this will be the closing scene in this war, as it was of the Old Revolutionary War of 1776."13

Chapter IV
"Oh this poor forlorn country."

Upon landing on the Peninsula the Eighty-third made a reconnaissance to Big Bethel, where a rebel outpost was thought to be stationed in advance of the main Confederate line at Yorktown, some twenty-five miles distant. The reconnaissance was brief and bloodless.

On the 2nd of April, General McClellan arrived at Fortress Monroe, and on the 4th, all six divisions of the army took up the march for siege lines near Yorktown. The Eighty-third Pennsylvania and Lieutenant Colonel Vincent prepared fortifications and one biographer later noted, "There was no soldier who worked harder in this siege."1 Vincent frequently commanded pickets for two or three miles along the line, and often had charge of work details in the trenches. In addition to performing the duties for which he was detailed, Vincent made the siege of Yorktown a study. He knew the position and the importance of every work and gun emplacement along the line. The shelling at Yorktown was his baptism of fire. Faced by overwhelming numbers, the Confederate forces withdrew from

Yorktown and the expected climactic battle did not materialize.

Marching up the Peninsula after the Confederate evacuation, McClellan's army reached the right bank of the Pamunkey River. Here Brigadier General Fitz John Porter, now commanding the newly created Fifth Corps, selected Vincent to take command of a small body of troops in a reconnaissance across the river in the lower part of King William County. No armed Confederates were found and this affair was bloodless.

By the third week of May the Army of the Potomac was nearing the gates of Richmond, but in a dangerous position. McClellan's army was divided: the Fifth Corps -- 27,000 men strong -- was on the north bank of the rain-swollen Chickahominy River while the rest of the army was south of the river.

Reaching the Chickahominy, the Eighty-third encamped near Gaines' Mill, twenty miles outside Richmond, and for several weeks did picket duty in the miasmic swamps through which the river flowed. Disease was soon to take its toll on the soldiers.

During the night of May 26th, Colonel McLane called the company commanders together and informed them to have the men ready to move at daylight. The regiment moved out before daybreak on the 27th, just before a heavy rain began to fall, and joined up with the rest of the division on the Mechanicsville Road. The men pressed on through the torrential rains. "After a fatiguing march of about eighteen miles," one soldier later wrote, "we came within a few miles of Hanover Court House, and before we had arrived fairly on the field, the cannonading commenced between our artillery and that of the enemy."2

As the men of the Eighty-third struggled through the dense undergrowth, Colonel McLane went ahead and encouraged the exhausted men to follow him, "Now is the time," said McLane, "to prove yourselves soldiers!"3

A veteran of the Eighty-third described the next scene: "The woods were three quarters of a mile in depth; and all the while we were marching through it, the heavy firing in front continued; and, as we approached the opening where the battle was raging, the crash of small arms and the roar of artillery became nearer, clearer, deadlier. As every fresh regiment came up to the support of our troops, we could hear them pouring whole broadsides at once into the ranks of the enemy, till finally the firing slackened; and, at the very moment we debouched from the woods, it entirely ceased."[4]

The battle drew to a close just as the Eighty-third came up to the battleline. For them, the fight at Hanover Court House was a brief but exciting battle. They suffered eight men wounded, and easily captured 118 Confederates.

A veteran of the fight wrote of the aftermath:

> The arrival of the French Princes of the House of Orleans, who were on the staff of General McClellan on the field, brought hearty and warm congratulations to General Butterfield and the Brigade. It had fulfilled the expectations and promise founded on its training and preparation, and the spirit and patriotism of the entire command, from its loved commander down to the humblest camp follower, teamster or clerk. There was a feeling of satisfaction and pride throughout the command hard to describe by any language. The Field Officers of the Brigade (all the mounted officers), assembled in groups after nightfall, and discussing the affair, resolved to present General Butterfield a pair of golden spurs in recognition of his having gallantly won his spurs in that first splendid fight with his Brigade. A committee was appointed and General Strong Vincent, then Lieutenant-Colonel of the Eighty-Third, was entrusted with the duty, and subsequently made the presentation.[5]

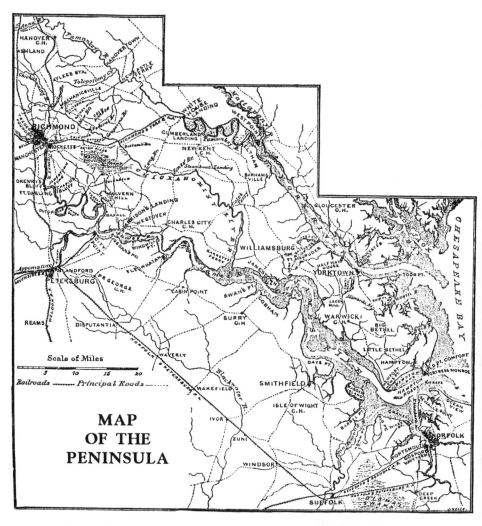

MAP
OF THE
PENINSULA

General Daniel Butterfield's golden spurs, presented by Lieutenant Colonel Vincent.

Elizabeth, at home in Erie with the Vincent family, constantly worried about and prayed for her husband. In a letter written on June 14th, Miss Porter's thoughts were of Lizzie: "It is no little thing for her to wait with submissive patience for the end of this campaign."6

During the third week of June 1862, Vincent was prostrated by "Chickahominy Fever," an often-deadly combination of typhoid fever and malaria. He convalesced at the army medical station less than a day when General Porter's Fifth Corps was attacked at Gaines' Mill. As the sound of far-off cannon and musketry reached the feverish Vincent, he tried in vain to learn the fate of his regiment. The news that the Eighty-third had been cut to pieces was kept from Lieutenant Colonel Vincent as long as possible; out of 550 men that entered the action, 265 were casualties. Colonel McLane and Major Naghel were both dead on the field. Summoning all of his waning strength, Vincent compelled a hospital attendant to bring him a horse. The next morning found him at Savage Station, now in command of his decimated regiment.

Vincent's energies were short-lived, however. He was soon overcome by fever, toppled from his horse, and was carried unconscious from the field on the back of a faithful orderly, John Hickey. Vincent later would remember nothing until he woke up halfway down the James River on board the hospital transport steamer *Spaulding*.

What Vincent did remember, with profound gratitude, was the attention of a kindly nurse, whose identity remains undiscovered, assigned to transport duty. It was through her efforts that B.B. and Lizzie were notified of the situation, and they were waiting for the transport when it landed in New York. The next three weeks were spent in Jersey City where Vincent's survival continued in doubt. Only by late July was he strong enough to make the journey home to Erie to recover.

Back on the Peninsula, the remnants of the Eighty-third held
an election to fill the vacancies created by the deaths of Colonel
McLane and Major Naghel. Though absent, Lieutenant Colonel
Vincent was elected Colonel and commissioned to date from June
27th, the date of the battle of Gaines' Mill.

On August 7th, the Vincent family physician, Dr. Brandes,
reported that the patient was "much reduced and is quite feeble,
being able to sit up only a small portion of the time. His present
disease is blennorrhea vesicae and of a severe character, and is
a great waste upon his system." Vincent's infection had spread
to the kidneys, bladder, and urinary tract.[7]

In a letter to Sarah Porter, Lizzie detailed the story of
Strong's sickness:

My dear Miss Porter,

I hardly have the time or the energy to tell you how
sorry I am and how guilty that I have not written to you
before. But when I tell you all about it, I know you will
not reproach me. Though I had not heard a word from
you during all these trying days and weeks till I reached
here and found your letters written long ago, still I knew
I had your sympathy, and I leaned on it. Each day and
night I thought of you, and often Strong was able to listen,
I tried to talk to him quietly and sweetly of you &
Farmington. If you could have seen how often the tears
would come as he tried to recall some of those old loved
days, you would know how we both love you. But let
me tell you something of what I have been through. I
have but little time.

I was in Cleveland when the first accounts came of the week's fighting. It was then that I heard of the Colonel's death and Father's departure for Fortress Monroe. I waited there from hour to hour in a state of anxiety that I don't want to think about now. Still I was quiet. Mary Atwater and her mother were ever so lovely. At last and suddenly came the summons home that Strong was sick. I had but an hour or two to be ready in. Mary promised me faithfully to write to you and tell you all that I knew. I could not write to anyone myself.

This was Friday. I could not find out anything definite at home, only that he was sick with camp fever. Saturday came and the report was confirmed in two ways--and that afternoon came the intelligence that he had been left and taken prisoner. A letter came now from a classmate saying that he was at McClellan's headquarters.

You know, Miss Porter, how very bitterly I suffered. But God was kind, and that evening came a dispatch from Fortress Monroe, telling me to meet him in New York on steamer Spaulding and signed by my husband. A more joyful house you could not imagine. It was all we asked then that he was not a prisoner.

I left at midnight and reached New York Monday morning. Theron [Doremus] immediately took every measure to reach the Spaulding and receive him from the hospital. That afternoon he was brought to me--oh so desperately sick and weak! Father had not found him and was half frantically pursuing him. He reached us on Tuesday, having been at Harrison's Landing and wherever he could hope to find him.

The fever was broken when he reached Jersey City. But then began a slight trouble with the urinary organs. After a few days of fever and only a little delirium he was better. I was much worn out without sleep or food. But you know I could not leave him till I knew he was better.

He was a perfect child in everything. He knew but little about all the fighting--remembered that the Colonel was killed and just one or two other circumstances. He knew nothing of his having taken command of his regiment and leading it a mile and a half after the Colonel's death in a state of perfect delirium. If it had not been for Gen'l. Porter and his faithful John, he never would have escaped, for he was so sick, they say, that he did not care himself what became of him.

O I want to see you to tell you all this! I am too tired to write.

Well, he improved rapidly for a week or so, when suddenly inflammation and hemorrhage of the bladder took place. His urine had been taken from him for two days after he reached N.Y.-- but when nature began to act itself, I certainly think I never saw such agony. His whole frame would just sway with pain, and the cold perspiration stream off him. Leeching subdued apparently the inflammation, for the hemorrhaging ceased.

His improvement was very slow then. The Dr. had to keep him very quiet. But at the end of last week the Dr. said we might come home. Theron and Sarah took us far as Albany. He seemed very bright there and quite strong. But oh what a skeleton he looked like!

The second day we rode from Albany to Buffalo, which was very wrong. But he took it in his head to do it & he is so weak that it is very hard for him to be opposed in anything. I feel sometimes as if it can hardly be my lovely Strong when I am nursing him, and then there will come times when he is tenderly sweet to me. He is patient and says God will be right to make him suffer a great deal of pain & that he is willing to give him his own time.

When we reached home, the crowd at the depot who were there to see him -- the delight at seeing his mother and sister and home--all were with his journey too much for him. Still I felt that rest would restore him, but on Sunday Dr. Brandes came and -- oh it almost breaks my heart to tell you what he said.

He feels that Dr. Zabriskie was deceived and that there is a disease of the whole urinary organs that is most critical. He told me that Strong is a perfect wreck and that he hardly dare touch him lest he should make him worse.

For three days he has done nothing, but this morning he goes to work. He has been studying the matter deeply, and though it is a rare disease he says that now he is armed to meet it.

It will be months before he can go into service, which just takes away all Strong's spirits, and the Dr. does not attempt to delude us that cure is certain. It may be that he will never be anything but a diseased man.

I will tell you plainly what I know of the truth. We are convinced that there has been a slight weakness there for years, but nothing noticeable. When he was at Yorktown and colonel of the trenches, he rode one of the McClellan saddles night and day for weeks. The result was that varicose veins were developed in the scrotum. He was then prostrated for two or three days with the most agonizing pain. Suspensory bandages relieved him. He wrote home of this, but not fully, and the Dr. says now that he would give forty thousand dollars rather than have him have this difficulty.

When the fever came on, by neglect during the retreat and on the steamer, these varicose veins extended up the neck of the bladder and how far and to what extent Dr. B. does not know yet, but his whole bladder and kidneys are evidently in a terrible condition.

Fever rises in the afternoon, and he is not so strong now as two weeks ago. He is not allowed to see anyone any more. Visitors on Monday -- especially some wounded officers of the 83rd -- Capt. [Hiram L.] Brown among them, who has just been released, perfectly overcame him. He cries like a child at the least occurrence that moves his feelings. I am so glad that I seem to be able to soothe & quiet him more than anyone else.

The Dr. this morning goes to work. He says that we must look for improvement by the month and not the week. I feel great confidence in him.

I feel happier today too -- yesterday I began to write to you, but sleepless nights, diarrhea, and anxiety made it impossible. I am stronger though than anyone would expect from what I have been through.

I believe God has answered my prayers to give me strength to take care of him. Mother of course takes some -- as Sarah did in Jersey City. Oh Miss Porter, that sister of mine is growing very lovely.

How God leads us to his will! This is a great, great lesson to Strong and me. I hope we may study it and improve by it, just as God wants us to. I believe it is to bring Strong to meek dependence on him, instead of his own energetic manliness -- and to make me more and more willing to put this husband in his hands. Just think how I wanted him home, and now to think I have him here -- but how? Oh I would be willing to let him go back tomorrow & never murmur if he was only well. So God leads us.

School closes probably this week. I cannot be denied your visit. I need it -- you do not know how much. It would do Strong good. The Dr. lets him go to the table and will have him taken out to ride, and he can talk quietly with us every day. Oh my precious Miss Porter, do come! We should all be so glad to see you. Strong lies on the bed -- he says give all my love to her -- and then adds I am too hot to send anything else today.

I am glad for Mrs. Richards. I could write all day, but there is so much to be seen for Strong that I must stop.

I have written in pencil, for I have had to pick up my paper anywhere I could get a chance.

Oh this poor forlorn country -- I can't write about it. Things are desperate, and I cannot but feel as Dr. Brandes says, that it is a very bad concern. I am glad that Strong is too weak to fully appreciate it. I believe it would craze him.

How we have wanted mind -- but we are now on the eve of something tremendous.

Do come to me--don't refuse me! I shall look for you soon. Forgive me for neglecting you.

Always yours,
Lizzie 8

After months of slow recuperation, a fully recovered Colonel Strong Vincent left Erie on October 1, 1862, traveled to the Army of the Potomac's encampment near Sharpsburg, Maryland, and assumed command of the Eighty-third Pennsylvania.

Both commander and men were elated to be together once more, though sorrow was mingled with Vincent's joy as he looked upon the thinned ranks and battle-torn flags. The regiment became strengthened by the arrival of recruits and convalescents, and during the mild October weeks he brought the Eighty-third up to its previous standard of excellence. The Third Brigade itself was also strengthened. The Twentieth Maine Regiment, commanded by Colonel Adelbert Ames, added over 900 men to the brigade. Still in the brigade was the Twelfth, Seventeenth and Forty-fourth New York and the Sixteenth Michigan.

On October 26th, the Army of the Potomac, nearly idle since the battle of Antietam in mid-September, crossed the Potomac River into Virginia. The slow-paced pursuit of the Rebel army brought an end to the controversial military career of George McClellan. President Lincoln elevated Major General Ambrose Burnside to command of the army on November 7th. General Butterfield replaced General Porter as commander of the Fifth Corps.

The Army of the Potomac was positioned near Warrenton for a week while Burnside prepared for direct action against General Robert E. Lee's Confederates at Fredericksburg.

On the morning of November 26th the army reached Aquia Creek at a point thirteen miles north of Fredericksburg and encamped near what later became known as Stoneman's Station. Burnside's plan was to cross the Rappahannock River, capture Fredericksburg and get between Lee's army and Richmond. The Eighty-third laid out its camp in a pine grove near the railroad that supplied the army.

As it became increasingly evident that a battle was imminent, the Vincent family became more concerned for Strong's safety. After hearing from a distraught Lizzie, Miss Porter wrote to a mutual friend on November 30, 1862:

"I have heard from Lizzie only once since her husband left her. I fear she is almost paralyzed by his absence, and indeed she seems to live more and more only in her enjoyment of him or her longing for him. I wish that they could live together in the ordinary routine of life."9

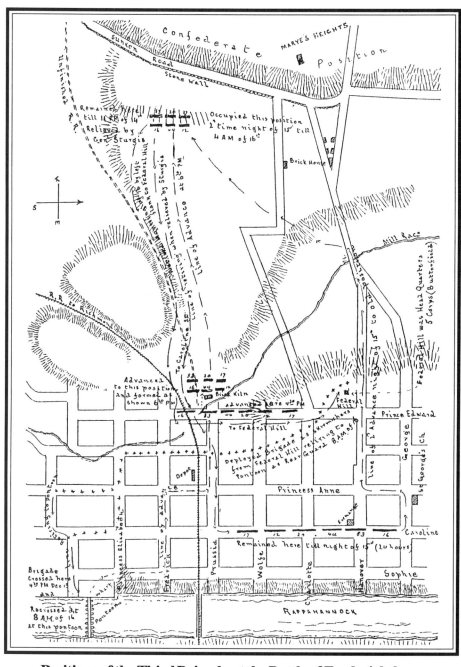

Positions of the Third Brigade at the Battle of Fredericksburg, December 13-16, 1862.

CHAPTER V
"There was not a waver of the line."

On the foggy morning of December 11th, the Federals began constructing pontoon bridges across the Rappahannock to Fredericksburg. Rebel troops occupied the streets and buildings of the town, and were also strongly positioned in the heights overlooking the city. From the buildings facing the river, Confederate sharpshooters from Brigadier General William Barksdale's Mississippi brigade were successful in driving the Union engineers away for a short time. At 10 a.m., Federal artillery on the east side of the river opened fire on the city, but were unable to dislodge the rebel marksmen from their positions. By late morning, only two bridges had been completed, but four Federal regiments had crossed the river by boat and driven out the Mississippians. On the Union left, troops under Major General William Franklin crossed the river in the afternoon, and a division belonging to Major General E. V. Sumner also occupied Fredericksburg by nightfall.

At sunrise on December 13th, the Third Brigade, under Colonel T. B. W. Stockton, came out of bivouac and stood under arms for three hours, while wave after wave of Federal infantry were slaughtered trying to capture the heights above Fredericksburg. At noon the brigade, including Colonel Vincent's Eighty-third Pennsylvania, began moving toward the pontoon bridges, and finally crossed at about 4 p.m.

A friend of Vincent later remembered him on that day: "Lying on the bank of the river opposite the city, he saw that he had a task before him that would require all his courage and all his nerve. His men were losing confidence and relish for fighting. When they crossed the river and passed through the town, upon the shelf of land back of the city, across which they had seen all day such desperate charges of our men to the foot of the semicircle of fortified hills, --and all in vain,--they felt that the battle of Fredericksburg was already lost."[1]

At about 4:30 p.m. orders came for the Third Brigade to advance.

Colonel Vincent's comrade noted, "It was now that Vincent proved himself. Before the battle the men of his regiment believed that he would prove a good leader. After it there was scarcely any position to which in their enthusiasm they would not have raised him."[2]

The Eighty-third stood in line of battle, its right flank resting on a railroad track fifty yards in front of a depot. On their left was the Sixteenth Michigan and further on their right was the Forty-fourth New York. Confederate artillery began to shell the Eighty-third's position and wounded a number of officers and men. Captain DeWitt McCoy of Company F was knocked senseless from the concussion of a passing shell. It was then that the Third Brigade was ordered to move forward and relieve the troops pinned down in the front line.

The brigade was reformed into an assault column. In the first line, on the left, was the Eighty-third Pennsylvania, the Twentieth Maine in the center, and the Seventeenth New York on the right. In the second line, the Sixteenth Michigan was on the left, the Forty-fourth New York in the center, and the Twelfth New York on the right. Vincent was ordered by Colonel Stockton to take control of the left wing of the brigade -- the Eighty-third, Forty-fourth, and Sixteenth. At 5 P.M., the Eighty-third rose up and advanced rapidly, gaining the crest of the hill in front of the enemy's right center batteries. "At that moment," Vincent wrote, "their guns opened upon us, with great briskness."3

An officer of the Eighty-third later wrote: "Here it was that Colonel Vincent first began to give indications of that bravery for which he afterwards became distinguished. With sword in hand he stood erect in full view of the enemy's artillery, and though the shot fell fast on all sides, he never wavered nor once changed his position. It was not rashness that inspired him, but a high and chivalrous sense of duty." 4

During the battle, the two left companies of the Eighty-third became separated from the rest of the regiment. Their advance became obstructed by a railroad embankment and a fifteen foot-deep ditch, which was filled with cowering men from the previously failed assaults. Vincent halted his line, brought the two companies back into position, and continued to advance.

"The storm of shot and shell and musketry that now poured into us was exceedingly destructive," Vincent wrote in his official report, "Officers and men fell rapidly, but there was not a waver of the line." Vincent was directed to take position at a small white house near the front of the rebel line. Reaching the foot of a slope, Vincent wheeled his regiment to the right, under a steady fire of musketry and a cross-fire of artillery. This was "handsomely accomplished," according to Vincent.5

One veteran of the Eighty-third later wrote of the assault: "In an instant we were up in line. The enemy saw us, and again let fly with redoubled fury the contents of their batteries upon us. Col. Vincent gave the command 'forward Eighty-Third!' and went ahead, sword in hand. We attempted to march straight to the front, in regular line of battle, but the buildings and fences opposed such insurmountable obstacles that we had to double up and march by the flank till we had cleared them. This threw us into confusion. We gained the open ground, however, and in a few moments were again in line pressing forward to the charge. This we did in the face of a murderous artillery fire."[6]

The Pennsylvanians steadily advanced toward the enemy. The combined effects of rough terrain, noise, and confusion repeatedly threw the ranks into disorder, but Colonel Vincent and his officers quickly reformed the line and the men pressed on. "My company officers held their commands well in hand," said Vincent.[7]

An officer of the Eighty-third wrote, "On we went, over the bodies of the slain, for a quarter of a mile, when we reached the brow of a hill a few hundred yards from the enemy's lines, and there halted. The position we had gained exposed us to an enfilading flank fire from the rebel batteries on our left. We had not been there but a few minutes before they opened, and for nearly an hour we laid close upon the ground and gazed upon their fiery messengers of death screaming over us."[8]

The men of the Eighty-third had commenced firing the moment they gained the hill, but as no enemy could be seen through the smoke and growing darkness, Vincent ordered the men to cease fire and conserve their ammunition. Some of the men had accidentally fired into the rear of the Twenty-fifth New Jersey pinned down in their front. Vincent ordered his command to move by the left flank, around the crest of the hill and form on the New Jersey regiment's left flank. All that could be seen of the enemy were the flashes of their muskets.

When the firing eventually diminished, Vincent took advantage of a slight rise in the ground and had his men further entrench themselves with earth thrown up by bayonets and tin cups. They were but twenty yards from the Confederate line. Vincent sent an aide to find General Griffin to request orders. When the aide returned, unable to find the general, Vincent threw out one company to his front as vedettes. The Eighty-third Pennsylvania would be pinned down in front of the Confederate line for the next twenty-four hours.

All day Sunday, December 14th, Vincent's troops lay in position behind their makeshift emplacements. The anticipated renewal of the assault was called off, and there was no further communication with army command. The brigade could not be moved from their perilous position and the men suffered greatly from the cold. One officer remembered that they "were so near the enemy that it was death to rise from the ground."[9]

An officer later recalled Vincent's coolness on that dreary night:

> Soon after sunset a message was sent out from the city for him to fall back as soon as he safely could. The men were immediately cautioned to be ready to rise and march to the rear. All knew the danger. The moon was shining brightly, and for an hour it seemed that it would be impossible to retire without loss of life. But when the order first came the young commander had observed a few little clouds just appearing over the hills. Soon those near him, wondering why he did not direct the movement to begin, saw his anxious look fastened upon one of these clouds; and as by inspiration the whole brigade knew what he was awaiting. The cloud increased in size, came nearer, grew blacker, came where all wished it would

come; and when at last the moon withdrew her face, for once unwelcome, the relief that came to every soldier's mind was inseparably connected with confidence in his commander.[10]

The brigade fell back to the city and remained in the streets of Fredericksburg all day on the 15th. Suffering from the exposure of the past thirty-six hours, Colonel Stockton found himself "seriously unwell" and was induced by his surgeon to give up command. Colonel Vincent, next in rank, assumed command of the Third Brigade and on Tuesday, the 16th, he was ordered to withdraw the brigade across the river. This was "performed promptly and safely...without any further loss of life."[11]

A tired veteran of the Eighty-third wrote, "With many a weary step and many a groan, up the high hills, leading back from the shores of the Rappahannock, we heaved ourselves like huge round stones; and, on reaching their summit, we turned and cast a farewell glance upon that place of skulls, where so many of our companions in arms lay stretched in the gory embrace of death."[12]

The Eighty-third suffered five men killed and thirty-two wounded at Fredericksburg. The defeated Army of the Potomac sullenly completed its withdrawal across the Rappahannock, with officers and men questioning both Burnside's sanity and ability. Lee's army was again triumphant.

On December 17th, in a letter to the Secretary of War, Fifth Corps commander General Daniel Butterfield recommended Strong Vincent for promotion to brigadier-general: "Col. Vincent has been long under my command, and has by gallantry and devotion to duty richly merited promotion."[13]

On January 22, 1863, a second attempt was made by Burnside to cross the Rappahanock and attack Lee. This time the plan was defeated by the weather when the Army of the Potomac literally became stuck in the mud. Ammunition wagons and supply trains became mired, and exhausted horses and mules dropped dead in their traces. The whole army was tired, wet, dispirited, and hungry. It was no longer a question of how to continue with the campaign, but how to get back to the camps opposite Fredericksburg.

The men of the Eighty-third returned to camp at Stoneman's Station and settled into winter quarters, knowing this would be the last "on-to-Richmond" movement until spring.

Colonel Strong Vincent

CHAPTER VI
"I enlisted to fight."

It was time to reorganize the beaten and demoralized Army of the Potomac. Changes were many. Lincoln removed Burnside as commander of the Army of the Potomac and placed Major General Joseph Hooker in command. Major General Daniel Butterfield became chief of staff, and Major General George G. Meade was placed in charge of the Fifth Corps. Brigadier General Charles Griffin remained commander of the First Division. Colonel Stockton continued as commander of the Third Brigade, although on several occasions, as senior Colonel, Vincent commanded the brigade in Stockton's absence.

Borrowing from Major General Philip Kearny's innovation of using a red badge to identify his soldiers, General Hooker ordered each corps to adopt an identifying symbol, hoping to enhance both organization and spirit. A red Maltese cross was designated as the symbol for the First Division of theFifth Corps.

During the army's winter encampment, Colonel Vincent

arranged for Lizzie to visit. A private in the Eighty-third, seeing the happy couple, remarked: "She was a very handsome young woman, tall, graceful, and a superb horsewoman. When his duties permitted, Vincent loved to ride with her through the camps of the army and about the surrounding country. They were followed with looks of admiration wherever they appeared. Their love was ideal."[1]

A friend of Vincent wrote of these halcyon days, "Many officers will remember Vincent's quarters near Potomac Creek, after the battle of Fredericksburg. He lived in the most homelike of tents; and, though he was not much given to visiting other officers, he had a way of drawing people to himself. He had much leisure, as the men of his regiment had been long in the field, and it required but little attention to keep them comfortable and in good drill and discipline, and his officers were competent and energetic. Therefore he was ever ready to extend a welcome to those who came. The quiet life of this winter was a taste of the life Vincent would have chosen. He was a soldier from a sense of duty, not from mere love of the profession, although he undoubtedly had the same enjoyment in a reconnaissance or a battle that he had felt in earlier life on a deer-hunt. But it would have been sweeter to him to sit in the door of his home."[2]

Another friend wrote, "As a general thing his companions were older than himself; for though Vincent was but twenty-five years old, he was already a little gray and quite stout; and this, with his decisive countenance and confident address, made him seem the compeer of men of forty. Among his associates were officers of the highest rank. He could adapt himself to all, -- could talk with the politician on questions of history, with a general officer on military evolutions, or with a sporting man on the relative merits of horses, -- and all repected his opinion."[3]

On January 24th, 1863, Vincent received a telegram from Lizzie mentioning an "important family matter." He immediately

Lizzie mentioning an "important family matter." He immediately requested a ten-day leave to be with her, and most probably learned upon his arrival that she was pregnant.

During the months of February and March, Colonel Vincent was assigned to general court-martial duties. So impressive were his legal skills that he was offered the position of Judge Advocate General of the Army of the Potomac. Vincent declined, partly because he considered the position below the status of regimental command, and partly because he could not abandon his beloved troops. "I enlisted to fight," Vincent said when friends pointed out the advantages of the staff position. He did, however, successfully defend Lieutenant Colonel Casper Trepp of the 1st U.S. Sharpshooters at his court martial. Trepp had been charged by Colonel Hiram Berdan of theft of regimental stationery -- a petty accusation made by the unpopular Berdan to oust Trepp from the regiment.[4]

Corps Badges of the Army of the Potomac under Hooker.

The flag presented to the Eighty-third regiment in April 1863 as a replacement for their battle-torn colors.

CHAPTER VII
"We must fight them more vindictively."

The advent of spring brought renewed Union confidence that the upcoming campaign would result in victory. In a letter to Lizzie, Strong wrote of the grim determination of the revitalized Army of the Potomac: "We must fight them more vindictively, or we shall be foiled at every step. We must desolate the country as we pass through it, and not leave the trace of a doubtful friend or foe behind us; make them believe that we are in earnest, terribly in earnest; that to break this band in twain is monstrous and impossible; that the life of every man, yea, of every weak woman or helpless child in the entire South, is of no value whatever compared with the integrity of the Union."[1]

On April 11th, the Pennsylvania Legislature passed a Joint Resolution authorizing a replacement color for the battle-torn flag of the Eighty-third. The veterans of the regiment were reluctant to give up the beloved banner they had followed in so many battles. Colonel Vincent received the new flag but not without some hesitation. He wrote, "a fresh, bright color assuming the place of the old one, makes them all look, the men say, like a new regiment. The sensitiveness is an honorable and a natural one, and I feel disposed, if possible, to gratify and respect it."2

On April 27th, the Army of the Potomac commenced what was becoming its annual movement towards Richmond, this time by way of Chancellorsville, fifteen miles west of Fredericksburg. On May 1st, Hooker announced, "The operations of the last three days have determined that our enemy must ingloriously fly, or come out from behind their defenses and give us battle on our ground, where certain destruction awaits him."3

On the morning of May 1st, the First Division marched eight miles to United States Ford. While on the move the regiment was ordered to halt, about face, and quick-time nearly back to their previous position. There they formed a line of battle in support of Regular troops already engaged with the enemy. After nightfall, the Third Brigade was ordered to take a position on the extreme left, so as to cover United States Ford and enable the balance of the army to cross over. An officer of the Eighty-third later wrote: "The woods through which we marched were on fire, the light of which and the rattling of our canteens gave the enemy notice of our movements and led them to open a brisk fire of musketry upon us."4

The Eighty-third pressed on through the thick underbrush and over the ditches and fallen trees. Vincent was ordered to follow the Seventeenth New York, but in the course of the march, three companies of that regiment had become separated from the rest and were proceeding in the wrong direction. The Pennsylvanians mistakenly followed these companies, and after groping and feeling their way through the woods for two miles, they came to a deep ravine. When rebels were discovered but a short distance away, Colonel Vincent realized they were on the wrong track. He threw out skirmishers on both flanks and in front, and rode off to find the headquarters of General Griffin to report the position of his regiment. With some difficulty Vincent found the General and was directed to bring his regiment, with the aid of a guide, to the Chancellorsville road. The Eighty-third reached its position at about ten o'clock, and rested for the remainder of the night.

The next morning, May 2nd, the Eighty-third rejoined the brigade and took a position on the left of the Fifth Corps' line of battle. Throughout the day the men busied themselves building timber-reinforced entrenchments along their portion of the line. On the morning of the 3rd they were relocated to a position near the right center.

Skirmishers were thrown out, and soon opened a brisk but short engagement with the enemy. Later, picks and shovels were distributed, and the men once again went to work digging fortifications. Throughout the day, and the next, the Eighty-third waited for an attack that never came. Some cannonading was heard to the left, and minor skirmishing continued. Since the Fifth Corps saw limited action, the Eighty-third Pennsylvania's losses were limited to five men wounded during the entire Chancellorsville campaign.

In the weeks that followed the failed Chancellorsville campaign the Third Brigade was reduced to four regiments. The Twelfth and Seventeenth New York were sent home when their terms of enlistments expired. As senior colonel, Vincent assumed command of the brigade upon Colonel Stockton's resignation on May 18th. One officer wrote of Vincent's capabilities, "His capacity as a commander and his bearing as a soldier had already made a favorable impression upon the officers and men of the whole brigade, and a general feeling of satisfaction was manifested at this change." He also wrote, "He soon proved himself to be the most popular brigade commander we had yet had; and, under his leadership , the famous old light brigade began to recover some of its former renown for discipline and soldierly conduct. "5

On May 22nd, Vincent, concerned about the health of his men in a worn-out campsite, ordered the brigade moved to a less crowded location two miles from Stoneman's Station.   One soldier wrote: "The indications were that we would stay there some time, and accordingly we went to work, turnpiking the streets, erecting bowers of pine and cedar and making various other preparations for the cleanliness and comfort of the camps. "6 While these comforts were still being prepared, the brigade was ordered to strike its tents and move farther up the Rappahannock to guard the fords.   After a short march, Colonel Vincent assigned each regiment of the brigade to a position. The Forty-fourth New York was stationed at Bank's Ford; the Sixteenth Michigan at a milldam a little further upriver; the Twentieth Maine at United States Ford; and the Eighty-third Pennsylvania at Richard's Ford.

The brigade remained posted for a week until it was relieved. It was then ordered to join for picket duty at Kemper's Ford, a few miles upriver. The opposing armies spent the first two weeks of June carefully watching each other from their opposite shores. When rebel sightings grew more scarce, Colonel Vincent crossed the river with two companies of the 16th Michigan on a reconnaissance. As was suspected, no enemy could be found. Lee had silently slipped away with his army to the west, and was now marching northward toward Pennsylvania.

CHAPTER VIII
"Stop that damned battery howling!"

General Hooker and the Army of the Potomac were now in pursuit, and on the 13th of June the Fifth Corps broke camp and headed north. The Third Brigade camped that evening at Morrisville, and Vincent invited Lieutenant Colonel Joshua Chamberlain and General Adelbert Ames to dine with him. The following morning Vincent's Brigade marched to Catlett's Station, then on to Manassas Junction, where they remained for two days. Lee's objective was still unknown and by Presidential order it was necessary for the Army of the Potomac to keep itself positioned between Lee's army and Washington. The Confederates continued north along the Blue Ridge Mountains on the west, followed by the Federals moving along the Bull Run Mountains about sixteen miles to the east.

through clouds of dust beneath a scorching sun. One veteran wrote of this experience, "On this march the men sweating beneath the heat and burden of the knapsacks, fell out in crowds and could be seen lying along every little stream, where a drop of water could be found to quench their raging thirst, or a bush to shelter them from the rays of the burning sun."1 The brigade rested at Gum Spring until the 19th, and then marched eight more miles to Aldie.

On June 20th, Union Cavalry commander Major General Alfred Pleasonton reported he had skirmished with rebel cavalry under Generals Jeb Stuart and Wade Hampton at Aldie, and had driven them back toward Middleburg. At midnight, Vincent was directed to report for instructions to Pleasonton at the Berkeley House just beyond Aldie. At three o'clock in the morning of the 21st, in the pouring rain, Vincent's Brigade was roused from sleep, and moved toward Middleburg to support an anticipated cavalry attack.

Vincent's Brigade engaged the enemy at Middleburg just after six o'clock that same morning, taking a position on the left of Major General David M. Gregg's cavalry division on Ashby's Gap Road. The rebel cavalry, fighting dismounted, were behind a series of stone walls adjacent to the south side of the road. A Confederate horse artillery battery of six guns, masked by a two-hundred-yard-wide belt of woods, was in position near the road.

At seven o'clock, Vincent was ordered by General Pleasonton to advance at least one regiment to dislodge the rebels from one of the stone walls. Vincent assigned the task to the Sixteenth Michigan, under Lieutenant Colonel Norval E. Welch. Vincent directed the Forty-fourth New York and the Twentieth Maine to simultaneously press the enemy hard and silence the battery's guns. The Eighty-third moved surreptitiously through the woods on the left, engaging the enemy on the flank and rear.

Vincent's attack was entirely successful. Finding their

position untenable, the rebels fled in confusion. The Sixteenth Michigan advanced on the double-quick, compelling the Confederates to abandon "a fine Blakely gun."2

A correspondent of *The New York Herald* wrote of the action, "When Colonel Vincent gave the order to charge on the battery it was not in precise military phrase, but 'stop that damned battery howling,' -- an order of such terse meaning and intelligibility as to be looked for from such a man."3

Vincent's Brigade now moved forward with Pleasonton's troopers and continued to dislodge the enemy from other stone walls. At Comeil's Run, the Confederates poured artillery fire on the brigade's exposed position, but Vincent's skirmishers forded the stream and again flanked the rebel line. The enemy then retreated four miles to Goose Creek.

Captain Amos Judson of Vincent's staff remembered the final assault:

> The banks of the creek at this point were high, steep and thickly wooded. The Eighty-Third had been ordered to ford the stream and again fall upon their right flank; but, as the depth made it impracticable, they again clambered up the bluff and came out into the road just in time to take part in the glorious affray that followed. The enemy were posted behind two stone walls; one at the foot of the bridge, and the other at the top and almost concealed by the tall growth of wheat through which it ran. The moment we came in sight both of these lines arose and poured a volley into our skirmishers. Now happened one of the liveliest and most exciting times we had ever yet experienced: when we were carried along, as it were, by the very tempest, whirlwind and, I might say, joy of battle into the midst of the enemy's ranks.4

Vincent's Brigade had driven the enemy six miles over

difficult terrain. Only exhaustion prevented the unmounted men from pursuing any longer.

Colonel Vincent, reporting on the final charge at Aldie, wrote, "The charges of the cavalry, a sight I had never before witnessed, were truly inspiring, and the triumphant strains of the bands, as squadron after squadron hurled the enemy in his flight up the hills and toward the gap, gave us a feeling of regret that we, too, were not mounted and could not join in the chase."5

Vincent had handled his brigade so skillfully that its total losses were two killed and eighteen wounded, a low casualty figure for a running fight of ten hours' duration. So impressed was Fifth Corps commander General Meade with Vincent's performance that he openly wished Vincent was a brigadier general in command of a division.

The fatigued brigade made its way back to Middleburg, and bivouacked on the Glasscock farm. Colonel Vincent and his staff used the house as headquarters for the night. "Oh dear," said Mr. Glasscock, "I wish this thing was over with!" He went on to say that he had hosted Confederate Generals Stuart and Hampton earlier for dinner that day, and that he and his family had taken refuge in the cellar during the cannonading. Now, as he was serving meals to the Union officers, he seemed, "very anxious to receive greenbacks in payment," according to a staff member.6

During a heavy rainstorm on the evening of June 24th, the brigade joined up with the rest of the division on a return march to Aldie. On the 25th, the entire Fifth Corps began marching toward the Potomac. At Goose Creek it was necessary to build a makeshift bridge from trees and fence rails to facilitate crossing. The Corps passed through Leesburg, and forded the Potomac at Edward's Ferry, halting ten miles beyond on the 26th. There, within two miles of Frederick, Maryland, the Corps rested for two days.

During this encampment the troops learned that General Hooker had been replaced by General Meade as commander of the Army of the Potomac. One officer of Vincent's Brigade wrote, "This change of commanders was received with quiet but apparent satisfaction."7 Fifth Corps command was assigned to Major General George Sykes, and the First Division was to be temporarily commanded by Brigadier General James Barnes in the absence of Major General Charles Griffin.

In the final days of June it became clear that events were steadily rising to a climax. Lee was in Pennsylvania and the Union Army was moving north to challenge the Confederate invasion. The long march resumed on Monday, June 29th, passing through Frederick, and on Tuesday, the 30th, through the inspiringly-named villages of Uniontown and Union Mills. The latter had seen rebel cavalry leave just five hours previous to the brigade's arrival, and the citizens greeted the Union troops with loud cheers.

In what was perhaps his final letter to Lizzie, written about the 30th of June, Colonel Vincent wrote, "We move tomorrow for the Pennsylvania border. A general battle must ensue soon. Lee's fate is sealed!"8

View of Little Round Top (at left) and Big Round Top (at right) taken from the J. Weikert farm lane two weeks after the battle.
Vincent's Brigade paused near this location before advancing to Little Round Top.

CHAPTER IX
"Hold this ground at all costs!"

The Fifth Corps continued its march through Maryland from dawn to dusk on Wednesday, July 1st, and finally stepped over the border into Pennsylvania. Just before reaching Hanover around noon, Vincent sent orders to the rear for the Eighty-third's ceremonial elements to come forward. He ordered the flag unfurled, and, to the pomp and splendor of the drum corps and color guard, he reverently removed his cap, and said to his adjutant, "What death more glorious can any man desire than to die on the soil of old Pennsylvania fighting for that flag!"[1]

The march continued through Hanover, and later that evening, as the brigade approached the little village of McSherrytown, the erroneous rumor circulated that General

McClellan had been reinstated to command the army. The men, joined by local citizens lining the roadside, cheered and celebrated till near midnight, believing their commander, once again, was Little Mac.

The troops were awakened before dawn on Thursday, July 2nd, after less than three hours of sleep, and formed up to head for Gettysburg. They had been hearing the sounds of battle since Hanover -- now they were eager for a fight.

By seven o'clock Vincent's Third Brigade massed near Powers Hill, east of Gettysburg. By mid-afternoon, the entire Fifth Corps was moved to the left of the Union line for the purpose of supporting the Third Corps, whose commander, Major General Daniel Sickles, had taken it upon himself to move his troops far in advance of the Federal line.2

General Sickles' decision to form a salient has been an abiding source of controversy since 1863. He was uncomfortable with his Corps' location along Union lines, and sought authorization from General Meade to adjust his position. Sickles interpreted Meade's reply as sufficiently noncomittal to allow his advance. As the Third Corps moved toward the Emmitsburg Road, a rocky hill known as Little Round Top -- the tactical left of the Union line -- was left completely without defense.

Vincent was ordered to move his brigade west from Rock Creek to the George Weikert farm, then, in anticipation of joining the furious Third Corps battle in progress in the wheatfield of the Rose farm, marched south between two wood lines -- perpendicular to the present-day Wheatfield Road -- where the troops paused in a swale near the J. Weikert house. During a moment of presentiment, Vincent said, "To-day will either bring me my stars or finish my career as a soldier."3

Colonel Vincent and his bugler, Oliver Norton, who also carried the brigade flag, rode slightly to the south of the house, and surveyed the battlefield. Just ahead of them was the north face of Little Round Top, a 550-foot boulder-strewn hill, recently harvested of its timber. The southern and western end of Little Round Top sloped to form a valley. To the south of this valley the terrain rose again to form Round Top -- also called Sugarloaf and Big Round Top -- a thickly-wooded hill towering 116 feet higher than Little Round Top.4

Sometime earlier, General Gouverneur K. Warren, Chief Engineer of the Army of the Potomac, rode along Cemetery Ridge with General Meade. The generals separated, Meade riding with his staff towards the Emmitsburg Road to confer with the beleaguered Sickles, and Warren, accompanied by several young engineer officers, including Lieutenant Washington A. Roebling, Lieutenant Ranald S. Mackenzie, and Captain Chauncey B. Reese, riding onto the northern summit of Little Round Top. There he found a signal officer and a few assistants -- the sum total of Federal troops presently occupying that strategic hill.5

Warren knew that Meade had previously ordered Brigadier General Andrew A. Humphreys' Second Division of the Third Corps to occupy Little Round Top, and the Division, which had been moving to join General Sickles near the Emmitsburg Road, turned by the left flank to comply. However, Meade coutermanded the order when he considered the urgency of Sickles' predicament, and the Second Division retraced its steps to advance to the Emmitsburg Road.

Now, as General Warren stood with the little group of Federal soldiers, he instructed one of his orderlies to direct Captain James Smith's Battery, stationed to the west at a massive pile of boulders called Devil's Den, to fire a round into the woods where the signal officer thought he had seen rebel troops. The shot whistling over their heads caused the Confederates to stir, and the reflections from their weapons confirmed that a line of enemy infantry was in the process of surreptitiously outflanking

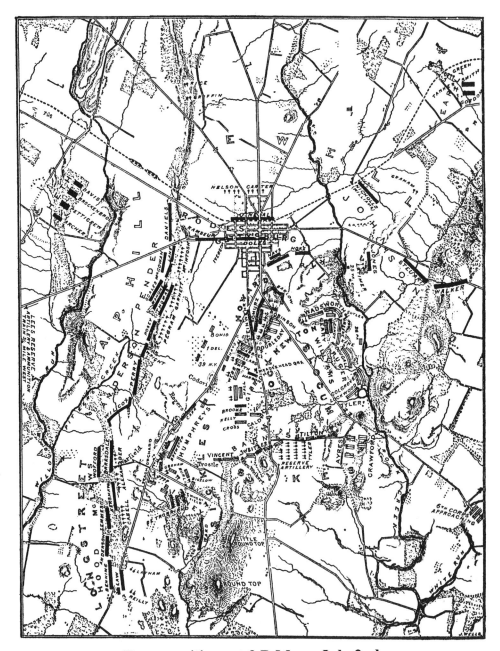

Troop positions at 3 P.M. on July 2nd.

the left of the Third Corps' First Division under Major General David B. Birney, which at that moment, was the extreme left of the Army of the Potomac.6

When General Warren realized the urgency of the situation, he sent one of his orderlies with a note to General Meade, asking that at least a division, hopefully General Birney's command nearby, be rushed to the defense of Little Round Top. When Warren realized Birney's troops were already engaged in battle, he sent Lieutentant Mackenzie to General Sickles, hoping he could spare a brigade. Sickles declined.

General Sykes, who had ridden forward toward the wheatfield to select a position for Barnes' division, was now approached by Lieutenant Mackenzie who conveyed to him the concerns of General Warren. Sykes agreed to send one of Barnes' brigades, and Mackenzie hurried back to Little Round Top to report this to General Warren. General Barnes, however, had separated from Sykes after initially riding forward with him to the wheatfield, and had not returned to his division's position.7

The conspicuous absence of General Barnes at this crucial time is an interesting element in the scenario which will bring Strong Vincent to his most glorious hour. In his official report, Barnes places himself with Sykes, scouting the wheatfield, when General Warren "came up, riding rapidly from the left," asking for assistance on Little Round Top. This is impossible, because Warren remained on Little Round Top until after Vincent's Brigade arrived. Sykes does not mention the incident at all either in his offical report or in future correspondence.8.9

Sixty-one year old Brigadier General James Barnes, Colonel Vincent's immediate superior, was a West Point graduate who remained at the academy as an instructor until his resignation from the army in 1836. He resumed his military career at the outbreak of war as colonel of the Eighteenth Massachusetts, and was promoted to brigadier general just seven months prior to the battle of Gettysburg. A book published in 1913 by a veteran of the Eighteenth Massachusetts details several instances in Barnes' career alleging bouts of intoxication.[10,11]

In 1910, Norton, in response to his publication of *Strong Vincent and His Brigade at Gettysburg*, received a letter from Corporal J.L. Smith of the 118th Pennsylvania Volunteers, 1st Brigade of Barnes' Division, accusing the General of drunkeness at Gettysburg. Smith said, "...in our haste to help Sickles we were hurried off to front.... General Barnes was on our left as we were marching out...and drinking out of a black commissary quart bottle.... Seems to me he was hollow from skull to boots."[12]

Years later, Norton wrote, "Barnes ought to have been where Vincent was, but I do not recollect seeing him at any time during the day, after the early morning. I was under the impression that Barnes was not in condition to command a division on the field of battle, and that Vincent knew it...."[13]

Vincent and Norton, waiting just ahead of their brigade, watched as Sykes' aide approached them at a gallop across the low ground from the wheatfield. As the aide drew closer, Vincent, with Norton just behind, rode forward to meet him. Vincent said, "Captain, what are your orders?" The officer responded, "Where is General Barnes?" Vincent again asked, "What are your orders? Give me your orders." The aide answered, "General Sykes told me to direct General Barnes to send one of his brigades to occupy that hill yonder," indicating Little Round Top. "I will take the responsibility of taking my brigade there," replied Vincent.[14]

Turning to Colonel James Clay Rice of the Forty-fourth New York, senior regimental commander, Vincent said, "Colonel, bring the brigade as quickly as possible on to that hill. Double quick where the ground will permit." Vincent and Norton then galloped off toward the northwest face of Little Round Top.[15] There they found the incline too steep and rocky to ascend on horseback, so they turned to the left and began to circumnavigate around the northern and eastern slopes. They found a more promising pathway near the south end, which borders the swale separating Little Round Top from Big Round Top, and they made their way upward and across toward the eastern ridge overlooking what would soon be known as the Valley of Death.

As the men, still mounted, halted near where stands today the Sixteenth Michigan monument, shells began to explode on either side of them. Vincent told Norton, "Down with that flag, Norton! D--n it, go behind the rocks with it!"16 Vincent followed Norton to the cover of a group of boulders, then dismounted and handed his reins to Norton, leaving his sword strapped to the saddle. Vincent then walked along the spur, selecting positions for the regiments of the brigade. The Forty-fourth New York led the column, followed by the Sixteenth Michigan, commanded by Lieutenant Colonel Norval E. Welch, then by the Eighty-third Pennsylvania, Vincent's former command, presently led by Captain Orpheus S. Woodward. Last in line was Colonel Joshua Lawrence Chamberlain's Twentieth Maine.

As each of the four units arrived, the commanders dismounted, leaving their horses with orderlies at the rear of the ledge. As the Forty-fourth New York approached their anticipated position, Vincent told Colonel Rice, "Form your regiment here, Colonel, with the right against this rock." Rice said, "In every battle in which we have been engaged the Eighty-Third and Forty-Fourth have fought side by side. I wish it might be so today." Vincent understood. He instructed the Sixteenth to pass, and occupy the right of the line. The Sixteenth Michigan, facing west across the valley below, was joined to the right of the Forty-fourth New York, which also faced west. The Eighty-third Pennsylvania came next, occupying the bend along the ledge, which required the right of its line to face west, then gradually turn southward. The Twentieth Maine continued the line in this direction, then

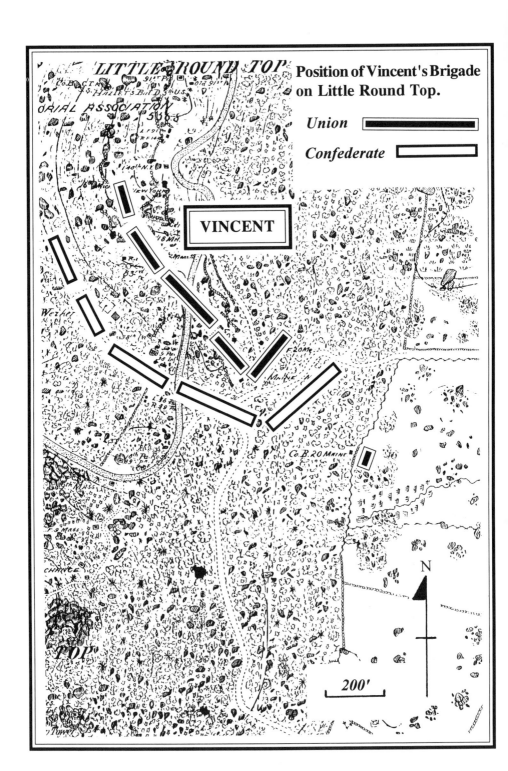

Position of Vincent's Brigade on Little Round Top.

Union
Confederate

The Twentieth Maine continued the line in this direction, then it also bent to cover the eastern exposure.

Vincent knew well the strategic importance of this ground, and he knew the tremendous danger his brigade would soon face in the effort to hold it. When Vincent positioned the Twentieth Maine, Colonel Chamberlain thought he spoke "with a voice of awe, as if translating the tables of the eternal law." To Chamberlain, Vincent said, "I place you here! This is the left of the Union line. You understand. You are to hold this ground at all costs!"[17]

Just before the impending attack, Vincent ordered a staff officer, Captain Eugene A. Nash, to "take a mounted orderly, go up on that bluff and observe the movements of the enemy." Vincent turned to Adjutant John M. Clark and said, "Go and tell Gen. Barnes to send me reinforcements at once; the enemy are coming against us with an overwhelming force."[18] Vincent then ordered another aide, Captain Amos Judson, to bring up more ammunition. Even bugler Norton left his horse and flag behind some rocks, grabbed a musket, and took a place in the line.

In the meantime, General Warren, still on Little Round Top, was unaware that his urgent plea for troops had been answered by Vincent, whose brigade had come up the hill to the rear and considerably south of Warren's position. He believed that Battery D of the Fifth U.S. Artillery, under Lieutentant Charles E. Hazlett, was the first unit to reach the threatened hill. The battery had begun to position itself near the signal station, when Warren, whose throat had earlier been grazed by a minie ball, left the hill in search of available infantry. Near Wheatfield Road he came across the Second Division's Third Brigade, which had formerly been Warren's command, now under Brigadier General Stephen H. Weed. The 140th New York, headed by Colonel Patrick O'Rorke, was detatched by Warren and guided up the northern slope of Little Round Top.[19]

Brigade was ferociously attacked by elements of Major General John B. Hood's Division, these being the Fourth and Fifth Texas under Brigadier General Jerome B. Robertson, and the Fourth, Fifteenth, Forty-seventh, and Forty-eighth Alabama regiments, under the command of Brigadier General Evander M. Law.

The 140th New York rushed along the slope of the hill toward the deafening noise of the struggle, and, as he gallantly led his troops into the thick of the fray, Colonel O'Rorke was struck by a Confederate bullet through the neck, killing him instantly.[20]

The 140th New York, despite the loss of their colonel, took up a position which joined them to the threatened right flank of the Sixteenth Michigan, occupying one of the most vulnerable positions of the tenuous line. They were soon joined by the Ninety-first Pennsylvania, the 146th New York, the 155th Pennsylvania, and General Weed himself. Later, as Weed stood near the artillery battery, he was struck through the spine by a minie ball, paralyzing him from the waist down. Lieutenant Hazlett, kneeling beside the mortally wounded General, was killed instantly when a bullet crashed through his head.[21]

The eleven hundred men of Vincent's Brigade desperately fought off increasingly fierce attacks by superior numbers of rebel troops. At the height of the most vicious assault, the colors of the Sixteenth were ordered back by Lieutenant William Kydd, who later claimed to have merely been relaying orders from his superiors. This act was the primary cause of a break in the Sixteenth's defense. From his vantage point just behind the Eighty-third Pennsylvania's right flank, Colonel Vincent watched as the men of the Sixteenth came into view falling back to the rear of the Forty-fourth New York. He rushed to the summit to stem the rout carrying only a riding crop, as his sword was still strapped to his saddle.

Near the top Vincent saw Sergeant Charles E. Sprague of

the Forty-fourth New York, who had been shot in the left shoulder.   Sprague, enroute to the rear to seek medical assistance, found himself in the middle of the Sixteenth's retreat. Years later, Sprague described the confusion:

> I turned toward them and commenced to exhort them to stand....   I was bleeding profusely and very likely a little delirious; my waist belt had broken and I was trying to hold up both my trousers and my wounded arm. The men of the 16th stared at me curiously, but I think what they saw was someone behind me, Vincent, coming up on foot with his wife's little riding-whip in his hand. He touched me lightly with his left hand, saying, "That will do, Sergeant Sprague; I'll take hold of this." ...Vincent went to driving the men of the 16th back into line with the little whip and that was the last attitude in which I saw him.[22]

It was during that crucial moment that Vincent, standing on the summit bringing the panic-stricken troops back into line, made himself an ideal target for hundreds of Confederate muskets. Mounting a large rock, Vincent shouted to his men, "Don't give and inch, boys, don't give an inch!"[23] Seconds later, a bullet slammed into the left side of his groin, passed through it and lodged in his right thigh, breaking the bones in its path. The gallant Vincent collapsed to the ground.

As he was carried to the relative safety of his original position behind the Eighty-third, Vincent said, "This is the fourth or fifth time they have shot at me, and they have hit me at last."[24]

While the battle raged furiously around the fallen Vincent, the Confederate tide began to ebb. More Federal reinforcements arrived, and the exhausted rebel units began to withdraw. The Twentieth Maine drove away the last of the Confederates at bayonet point, pursuing them toward Big Round Top until they were recalled. Colonel Rice assumed command of the brigade, and Colonel Vincent was transported to the Fifth Corps field hospital in the Jacob Weikert farmhouse, on the reverse slope of Little Round Top. Later, when artillery fire jeopardized the location, Vincent was moved to the Louis A. Bushman farm, a mile farther to the rear.

Vincent's Brigade had held Little Round Top, but at an overwhelming cost.

CHAPTER X
"I presume I have done my last fighting."

After dusk, when the fighting had ceased, Colonel Rice directed Norton to mount up and ride to the rear, with his brigade flag as his symbol of authority, and return with as many ambulances as the Fifth Corps field hospital would allow. Norton found the task of locating the hospital difficult in the post-battle pandemonium, as he "found the whole country to the northeast of Little Round Top filled with field hospital tents, and ambulances coming and going...." None of the ambulances, he was told, could be re-routed without proper authorization, so his search continued with no success.

He was returning to Little Round Top when he saw Colonel Welch of the disgraced Sixteenth Michigan sitting on his horse, with his regimental colors and at least forty of his men nearby.

Welch, in an apparent attempt to mask the cowardice of his unit
in the face of the enemy, told Norton the regiment had been driven
from the hill, and, hoping to locate the rest of the brigade, had
followed Norton and his flag. "I think Welch and these men had
been skulking behind the high rocks," Norton wrote later, "and
followed my flag when they saw me go down the hill." Welch
then pointed to a nearby farmhouse, and told Norton he believed
Colonel Vincent was inside.

Norton knew Vincent had been shot, but had no idea as to
the severity of his wound. Norton dismounted, leaving his horse
and flag with one of the men of the Sixteenth, who told him he
didn't believe Welch's story about the brigade leaving Little
Round Top. The ever-faithful Norton then cautiously stepped
into the house.

Blood and bodies and the wounded were everywhere. He
found his Colonel, pale and barely able to speak, in a room on
the first floor. Vincent held out his hand to him. Norton grasped
it, and said, "The boys are still there, Colonel." Vincent smiled
contentedly, pressing Norton's hand tighter. Norton tried to
express his grief over Vincent's condition, but was too overcome
with the sorrowful scene before him. He hurriedly left the room.
Norton said, "That was my last sight of one of the most gallant
heroes of the war."[1]

On the morning of July 3rd, Major General Daniel
Butterfield, Chief of Staff of the Army of the Potomac, visited
Colonel Vincent, informing him that General Meade had earlier
telegraphed Washington for authorization to promote him to the
rank of Brigadier General. Vincent strained to ask Butterfield
for permission to go home to his family in Erie to recover, being
unaware that he was mortally wounded. Butterfield immediately
authorized two of Vincent's staff officers present to take their
wounded commander home. One of the staff officers later
remembered, "But on consulting the Brigade Surgeon, who came

in a few hours afterwards, he was told that his removal was entirely impracticable, and was advised to dismiss the idea at once from his mind."

"Then," whispered Vincent, "I want you to send for my wife as soon as possible."2

Adjutant Clark quickly mounted and rode to Westminster, twenty miles south, and telegraphed Erie. Another staff officer rode east to Hanover on the same mission. Due to the "confusion and press of business which prevailed," it wasn't until the evening of the 5th or morning of the 6th that the family learned of Vincent's injury. Strong Vincent's last wish, to have his wife by his side during his final hours, would regretably be unfulfilled. Elizabeth was seven months pregnant and in no condition to travel, but her father-in-law left immediately to be by his son in Gettysburg.

"In the meantime," wrote Captain Judson, "Col. Vincent kept slowly but gradually sinking away. He became conscious of his situation, but never uttered a groan nor complaint, and said repeatedly that he suffered no pain. The only times he suffered was when he was moved from one side to the other, and his broken limb was jarred by the operation, although it was handled with all the care and delicacy that it was possible to exercise. Even then he would surpress the outbursts of agony that his pain seemed to bring forth as if he thought the outward manifestation of suffering was unworthy a soldier and a hero."3

As Vincent lay dying he was visited by many comrades who came to bid him farewell and congratulate him on his impending promotion. Generals Sykes and Barnes were among the high-ranking officers who came to Vincent's deathbed.

"I presume," said Vincent, "I have done my last fighting."4

Vincent lingered on the brink of death through the long hours of July 6th. On the morning of the 7th it became evident that he was approaching his final hours. Captain Judson wrote,

"At that last moment a tender recollection of the Christian education he had received seemed to come over him, and while the feeble effort to repeat the Lord's Prayer was still lingering upon his lips the soul of this young hero passed away to another world."5

His body was most likely embalmed later that day. On July 8th, Adjutant Clark left Gettysburg for Erie with the earthly remains of General Vincent, unaware that B.B. Vincent was at that same hour enroute to Gettysburg. The elder Vincent finally succeeded in reaching the battlefield on the 8th, "after several days delay, owing to the crowd pressing that way and the interruption of some of the ordinary lines of travel consequent upon the rebel invasion."6   Searching for his son among the twenty-thousand wounded in and around Gettysburg was a heart-rending labor for the old man.   A correspondent for the *Erie Weekly Gazette* reported, "On arriving there he was informed by a soldier that Colonel Vincent had died on Tuesday and that his body was at that time being conveyed home. The intelligence of course fell upon his heart with crushing power, but burying for the moment his grief at the loss of a beloved son, he turned his attention to other members of the noble 83rd who had met a like fate in the conflict."7

Captain John Sell of the Eighty-third had been wounded by a shell fragment on July 2nd, died on the 3rd, and had been hastily buried. B.B. Vincent made inquiries regarding his wish to have the Captain disinterred, embalmed, and coffined, enabling him to return the body to Erie. The effort proved difficult for Mr. Vincent, as Captain Sell's body was in "an advanced state of decomposition,"8 and considerable time would be needed to prepare the corpse.   Mr. Vincent made the arrangements and quickly left for home to attend his beloved son's funeral.

Lieutenant Clark arrived in Erie with the body of General Vincent on Friday evening, July 10th.   The funeral was scheduled for Monday, July 13th, from the Vincent family home.

The *Erie Weekly Gazette* reported on Thursday, July 16, 1863:

> The fears which we expressed in our last issue regarding the fate of this gallant young officer have been realized. He died from the effects of his wound, and his remains were brought to this city for interment last Friday night in charge of Adjutant Clark of the 83rd Regiment. He was buried on Monday with the honors of war, and the melancholy and imposing obsequies will not soon be forgotten by those who witnessed them. A detachment of U.S. Regulars, which forms a part of the military force of the Provost Marshal of this District, was brought from Waterford to take part in the ceremonies. The hearse was neatly and appropriately trimmed, and told its own sad story with the Flag draped in mourning and the hat and sword of the brave and lamented dead whose "occupation's gone." The coffin was covered with black cloth, around which was wrapped the American Flag, with wreaths of flowers and evergreens, and having upon it a silver plate bearing the following inscription: ---

> COL. STRONG VINCENT,
> Died July 7th, 1863, of wounds received in the battle
> of
> Gettysburg,
> Aged 26 years.
> The following officers acted as bearers: Col. [LEWIS] GRANT, Col. [MATTHEW] SCHLAUDECKER, Lt. Col. [DAVID] McCREARY, Capt. T. AUSTIN, Lieut. [WILBERFORCE] LYON, and Lieut. EDWARD REED.

The procession moved from the residence of the father of the deceased to St. Paul's Church in the following order:

Detachment of Regulars,
Mehl's Band,
Artillery,
Hearsc and Bearers,
Horse, led by Attendants,
Guard,
Members of the Bar, Furnace Moulders, and Citizens,
Carriages.

Arriving at St. Paul's, the solemn and impressive burial service of the Episcopal Church was read and an address delivered by the pastor, Rev. J.F. Spaulding, calculated from its pervading spirit to console afflicted relatives and friends, bearing testimony as it did to the pure and noble character of the deceased, and the patriotism and gallantry which signalized his short but brilliant career.   At the conclusion of the service, the funeral cortege took up its line of march for the cemetery, where the concluding rites were performed, a volley fired over the grave, and the young hero was left to his last sleep.

The untimely death of General Vincent -- we call him General, because he was made such before his death -- has created profound sensation in this entire community. His patriotic devotion to his country, not less than his manly qualities of heart, had endeared him to all who knew him.   His abilities and bravery, demonstrated on many battlefields, gave him a reputation of which not his relatives alone, but the citizens of Erie County could well feel proud. The testimonials from his own favorite Brigade, especially, warrant us in saying that the memory of his noble traits will be cherished not less reverently than that of the courage and talents which gave him distinction as a soldier. "His death shall be the inspiration of the living who, like him, tread steadily the paths of patriotism and honor that point the way to imperishable renown."

Gen. Vincent entered the service with the three months Regiment organized here under the direction of Col. J.W. McLane and ordered to Pittsburg, in which he held the position of Adjutant. Immediately after its return and dismissal, the 83rd Regiment was formed with Gen. V. as Lieutenant Colonel. He succeeded to the first command after the death of Colonel McLane, participating in most of the battles fought by the Potomac Army, and in every case distinguishing himself by his gallant and heroic conduct. In the second day's contest at Gettysburg, he occupied a position of great difficulty and responsibility, and was mortally wounded in the act of urging forward his Brigade to effort and to victory.

Thus terminated the career, in the morning of life, of one of Erie's most gifted and promising sons. Highly educated, endowed with brilliant talents, generous-hearted, magnanimous and brave, he unhesitatingly met the demands of his country and fell in defense of its Government and its Institutions -- fell at the early age of twenty-six. -- While we lament his death, and condole with his bereaved and stricken wife, father, mother, brothers and sister, we yet point to his example as worthy of imitation by all "the truly noble" and patriotic.

The day before Vincent's funeral in Erie, Colonel Rice issued the following general order to the Third Brigade, now in pursuit of the retreating rebel army:

> July 12, 1863. General Orders No. 5}
> The colonel commanding hereby announces to the brigade the death of Brig.-Gen. Strong Vincent. He died near Gettysburg, Pa., July 7, 1863, from the effects of a wound received on the 2d instant, and within sight of that field which his bravery had so greatly assisted to win. A day hallowed with all the glory of success is thus sombered by the sorrow of our loss. Wreaths of victory give way to chaplets of mourning, hearts exultant to feelings of grief. A soldier, a scholar, a friend, has fallen. For his country, struggling for its life, he willingly gave his own. Grateful for his services, the State which proudly claims him as her own will give him an honored grave and a costly monument, but he ever will remain buried in our hearts, and our love for his memory will outlast the stone which shall bear the inscription of his bravery, his virtues, and his patriotism.
> While we deplore his death, and remember with sorrow our loss, let us emulate the example of his fidelity and patriotism, feeling that he lives but in vain who lives not for his God and his country.

Pregnant and distraught, Lizzie Vincent remained with the Vincent family in Erie. Her mentor, Miss Porter, confided in a letter to a friend that Lizzie "rather dreads to sleep as she often dreams of her husband's death."[9] On September 29th, ten weeks after the funeral, Elizabeth gave birth to nine-pound Blanche Strong Vincent. Miss Porter reflected on her friend's joy: "I hasten to send you the good tidings that Lizzie Vincent has a little girl. Mrs. Doremus writes that she was very ill, but is doing well. She says Lizzie's cheerfulness astonishes her that her affections are fixing with all the strength of her nature on the little one; that she does not seem disappointed that she has not a son and speaks of Strong's delight as if he were only absent on duty."10

Tragedy visited Elizabeth Vincent once again when her little Blanche died on September 20, 1864, nine days before her first birthday.

Lizzie would remain with the Vincent family for the rest of her days. When Strong's younger brother Boyd became an Episcopal priest and later a bishop, he continued to provide a home for his widowed sister-in-law. Years after the devastation of her husband's and daughter's deaths, Bishop Vincent wrote:

With her personal attractiveness and her rare intellectual gifts and culture, she was not only a constant inspiration to the younger members of the family and to a large social group of earnest young Erie people, but also threw herself with enthusiasm into all the church work in which the family was interested, conducting mothers' meetings and large bible-classes of working men, etc. After the family moved to Pittsburgh, she was a leader in the church work there, too, organizing forms of charitable work for young women and children, which still goes on there. So, too, when the family moved to Cincinnati, she led in the same kinds of work, and was at one time even the superintendent of the Sunday school of Grace Church, Avondale. In connection with such work she became much interested in sacred art; conducted for years an art-class for women; wrote two volumes, one on *Mary, the Mother of Jesus*, and the other *The Madonna in Legend and Art*; kept up her studies in French, German and Italian; and translated from the German, Delitzsch's *Behold the Man* and *A Day in*

German, Delitzsch's *Behold the Man* and *A Day in
Capernaum*. Her books of European travel and of art-
literature and the thousands of art-photographs she
gathered made a rare private collection of the kind. When
we moved finally into the large "Bishop's House"
provided by the Church, her intelligence and taste had
such full scope in its arrangement and adornment, that it
has even been spoken of as "a liberal education in itself."

One of the finest things in her life was her devotion
to and care of our defective and dependent brother Ward.
For fifty years she taught and trained him slowly, with
a patience often sorely tried, to get what little good and
happiness out of life was possible to him. Everybody
in the family connection loved her and "Cousin Libby"
was often called by them "the noblest Roman of them
all."[11]

More than fifty years after the death of her husband,
Elizabeth Vincent passed away in Cincinnati on April 14, 1914,
and was buried on Easter Sunday in the Vincent family plot in
Erie Cemetery beside her beloved husband and daughter.

In 1889, a monument to the Eighty-third Pennsylvania
Regiment was dedicated on Little Round Top. A bronze statue
of General Vincent, preparing to draw his sword, stands atop the
monument. As the gray-haired veterans looked on, Vincent's
flag-bearer, Oliver Willcox Norton, spoke:

The line was held, but at what a cost. Throwing
himself into the breach he rallied his men, but gave up
his own life. Comrades and friends, that was not a bauble
thrown away. In the very flower of his young manhood,
full of the highest promise, with the love of a young wife
filling his thought of the future with the fairest visions,
proud, gentle, tender, true, he laid his gift at his country's

altar. It was done nobly, gladly....

This place is holy ground....May we not reverently say that those who have gladly died for men are not dead, but are with us today; more living than when they stood to stem the tide of invasion. If we are proud to say that we were in that line on Little Round Top, can you think that they regret it? With clearer vision than ours their eyes see this broad land a nation...they look down the coming years and see it peopled with a host of free men, rejoicing in the result of their sacrifice.   They are content. 12

Eighty-third Pennsylvania Monument on Little Round Top.

Bronze likeness of Strong Vincent atop the Eighty-third Pennsylvania Monument.

For this portrait of Strong Vincent, made after his death, the lithographer removed the eagle from the shoulder strap and added a brigadier's star.

Colonel Vincent's shoulder strap cut from his uniform as a keepsake.

Strong Vincent High School, Erie, Pennsylvania, dedicated October 24, 1930.

APPENDIX I
Genealogical Background

Long before there was a Strong Vincent, there were the Strongs and the Vincents. The families, respectively of English Puritan and French Huguenot ancestries, were well acquanted with each other two generations before Strong was born. The first Vincents arrived in America about 1687, having fled from religious persecution first to England, and settled in New York City. Jean Vincent and his wife, Susanne, came with a contingent of family that included their eleven-year-old son, Levi. By the time Levi was in his late twenties or early thirties, he had relocated himself to Newark Township, Essex County, New Jersey. There he died at the family homestead in 1763 at the age of eighty-seven.

His son was John Vincent, born in 1709 on the family estate, who married Elizabeth Doremus. She was a Dutch girl who could not speak English, and John could speak no Dutch. Yet they communicated well enough to raise a family of nine children, among them Cornelius, born in 1737.

In 1772, thirty-five-year-old Cornelius set out with an extended assemblage of the Vincent family, including his parents, and began a homestead in Northumberland County, Pennsylvania, near the town of Milton. With him was his wife, Phebe Ward, with whom he would have nine children. In 1779, during the American Revolution, Cornelius and two of his sons were captured by a combined force of British infantry and local Indians, and were exiled to Quebec until the end of the war.

One of Cornelius and Phebe's sons was John, who was born on the family's New Jersey farm in 1772. At age twenty-five, left penniless by the effects of the Revolution, he settled at Fort LeBoeuf, now Waterford, Erie County, Pennsylvania. There he engaged in a mercantile and freight business between Waterford and the town of Erie, less than fifteen miles to the north. Five years later his finances had recovered sufficiently to permit his marriage to Nancy Boyd. That same year, despite a limited education, he was appointed Justice of the Peace, and, two years later, Associate Judge of the Court of Common Pleas of Erie County, where he served over forty years.

John Vincent made a fortune transporting the necessities of life in those days: salt, tobacco, and whiskey. He knew the value of a dollar well, but was exceptionally generous to family members. His children were expected to return to the old home in Waterford each Christmas, where they would each find a $100 bill under their dinner plate.

The eldest of the six children born to John and Nancy was Bethuel Boyd Vincent, born in 1803, who would become the father of Strong.

Strong Vincent's mother's genealogy is equally impressive. Her great-great-great grandfather was Elder John Strong, born in England in 1605, who arrived in America in 1630, just ten years after the Mayflower landed. His wife died either enroute or shortly after docking, leaving two young children, one of whom died two months later. That same year he took a second wife, Abigail Ford, and for the next fourteen years they lived in the Massachusetts settlements of Dorchester, Hingham, Boston, Taunton, and Plymouth. He then moved to Connecticut, and became a Supervisor of the East Windsor Colony there. In 1659 he relocated to Northampton, Massachusetts, although the three succeeding generations remained rooted in Connecticut. In Northampton he was ordained ruling Elder of his church, and retained this title for the rest of his days. In a lifetime that spanned ninety-four years, he had sired eighteen children distributed over thirty-nine fertile years.

His eldest son was John Strong, Jr. (ca. 1632-1698), whose wife Elizabeth Warriner gave birth to a son, Jacob. Sources differ over Jacob's vital statistics--he was born in either 1664 or 1673, and died in either 1740 or 1750. In 1719, he and his wife Abigail Bissell (1676-1749) became parents to Timothy, who fought with Connecticut troops during the American Revolution.

Timothy, who survived eighty-four years, fathered four children by his first wife, five by his second, and one by his third. The oldest of his second brood was Martin, born in 1770 to Abi Collins.

Martin spent his first twenty-three years on the family farm in Connecticut, then migrated to western New York, where for two years he worked as a land surveyor in the Genesee Valley. He then removed to Presque Isle, Pennsylvania, where he found a tent settlement consisting of two families, although nearby a contingent of surveyors and engineers were in the process of laying out the town of Erie. In 1795, he hired out as a laborer to one Colonel Seth Reed at wages of fifty cents a day. When time came for settlement, Reed told him that he was being charged seventy-five cents a day for board. In disgust, Martin shouldered

Rose Vincent (1847-1894), sister of Strong Vincent.

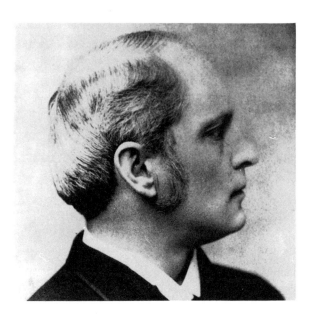

Boyd Vincent (1845- 1935), brother of Strong Vincent.

seventy-five cents a day for board. In disgust, Martin shouldered his knapsack and started off for Pittsburgh. He had gone only ten miles when he found himself attracted to the elevated land that a few families had established as Waterford the year before, and decided to settle there instead. In Waterford, two years later, he would meet and begin a generations-long friendship with John Vincent.

Martin was an enormously powerful man who cleared tracts of wilderness with the zeal of a true pioneer. When the Erie and Waterford Turnpike was subsequently routed past his house, he established a tavern and a tollgate nearby. He eventually expanded his holdings to eight hundred acres, and when he died in 1858, he was the largest property owner in all of Erie County, which had grown to a population of 50,000 souls.

His lifespan of eighty-seven years was highlighted by the founding of a school and a multi-denominational "Union Church" on his farm, and the donation of land for a public cemetery. He received a commission in the State Militia, and, for the rest of his days was addressed as "Captain."

His first wife, Hannah Trask, died in 1807 at the age of twenty-one years, leaving an infant daughter. Four years later he married Sarah Drake, a girl from his ancestral digs back in Connecticut, whose own distinguished parenthood included great Uncle Samuel Huntington, a signer of the Declaration of Independence. Martin and Sarah were the parents of six more children, the eldest of whom was Sarah Ann, born in 1812. She would become the mother of Strong Vincent.

Bethuel Boyd Vincent died on July 21, 1876, two weeks shy of his 73rd birthday. Strong's mother, Sarah Ann, was in her ninetieth year when she died in 1902. In 1924, Episcopal Bishop Boyd Vincent wrote *Our Family of Vincents*, a short history and genealogy of the Vincent family. He died in 1935 in Cincinnati. In his book he reflected on the loss of his noble brother, "The

Reed Vincent (1851-1873), brother of Strong Vincent.

death of so promising a man and so fine an officer, at such an early stage in his career, seems at first very mysterious. It looks, to our superficial human judgment, like 'a premature death,' like 'a life cut short.' And yet, even if he had lived out the ordinary term of human life, could he ever have served his country and his fellow men more worthily, could he ever have fulfilled himself more perfectly than in that one moment and act of supreme self-sacrifice for their sake?"

Sources

Vincent, Boyd. *Our Family of Vincents*. Cincinnati: Stewart Kidd Company, ca. 1924.

Dwight, Benjamin W. *The Descendants of Elder John Strong in America*. 1871. Reprinted by the Strong Family Association of America, 1975.

Drafts submitted to the Strong Family Association of America for 1992 update.

APPENDIX II
1862 Medical Condition

The following letters regarding Colonel Vincent's 1862 affliction with "Chickahomy Fever" are located in his service file.

The identity of Mr. Derickson, who apparently was acquainted with the Governor of Pennsylvania, remains a mystery.

Jersey City, July 21, 1862
Govr. Curtin

Dear Sir,
On my arrival here a few days since, I called to see Col. Vincent of the 83rd. Pa. Volunteers at his lodgings in this city, and found him quite ill. He is very anxious to return home where he thinks his recovery would be more certain, and in this I most certainly concur. He has no discharge and there being no military officer in command here, I have thought that you might interfere to have him allowed to return home for a____ period. I know of no other way to provide in his care. So as to get the ____ relief, will you be kind enough to get for him the necessary order and send it to him care of T.S. Doremus, 178 Reed St. New York. I have seen the attending physician of Col. Vincent and send you

his certificate of the nature of his complaints, etc. Your kind attention in this application will be most duly appreciated.

Very Respectfully,
David Derickson

Jersey City, July 21, 1862.

I have been attending to Col. Strong Vincent for the past two weeks as a practising physician. His disease_____of what is commonly called Camp fever, of which he is better, but his urinary organs are in a very diseased condition, and may require months before he will be able to return to active service.

Short of three months is by no means probable and the slightest amount of excercise will seem to aggravate the disease.

Dr. A. Zabriskie M.D.

APPENDIX III
A True War Story?

In 1912, a soft-cover book was published by David W.
Stafford, a veteran of Company D, Eighty-third Pennsylvania
entitled *In Defense of the Flag, A True War Story.* In it he presents
an account of an incident that allegedly occurred at Chancellorsville,
"just after the first and second battles of Fredericksburg:"

We had orders to get ready for a general inspection
of arms and all charges in the guns were to be withdrawn.
In front of us there was heavy timber, and perched in the
trees were many sharpshooters, ready to shoot any of our
men who raised their heads above the line of fortifications
that we occupied. We had orders to draw all the loads
from our guns and I had tried to obey but could not get
the charge in my rifle dislodged. I had to get a special
instrument, called a wormer, placed on the end of my
ramrod to take the ball from the gun. Well, I had got
one of these wormers fast in my weapon and I spoke to
my captain in regard to my firing the gun. He told me
that Colonel S. Strong Vincon [*sic*], our colonel, had
given orders for every man to draw the charge from his
gun and be ready for inspection, as they must fire their

guns. I told him what shape my gun was in and told him in order to unload it I would have to pick some powder and fire it in the fortifications, and did so. The colonel came very soon and looked at each gun close to where I was. Soon he took my gun and raised the hammer and blew in the nozzle. The smoke came out of the tube and he ordered me to climb on the fortifications there and remain two hours or until he would have me come down. This was supposed to be one of the rashest things that any of our commanding officers had ever done. Well, I had nothing else to do but to obey the colonel and I had no sooner gotten fairly on the line of the works than the enemy's sharpshooters commenced firing at me. Here is one place in my life where I knew that I was being fired at, and if there was one shot fired I believe there was thirty. Captain Woodard [*sic*] of our Company went right after the colonel and told him that he had command of Company D and he would either take that man from those works or either one or the other would die, and while they were contending over the matter I came down off the works. Well the next battle that occurred was at Gettysburg, in my own native state, and here the colonel was shot by sharpshooters and died in a few hours. Thus ends this thrilling experience.

A synopsis of the ridiculous elements in this tale would include the unlikelihood of Confederate "sharpshooters" missing their target thirty times, the inadvisability of a commander sentencing a soldier to death for firing his weapon, and the improbability of a colonel reversing himself at the insistence of a captain.

Fortunately for the memory of Colonel Vincent, the rest of the Stafford's book is an equally preposterous exaggeration of escape adventures and daring rescues that would be more suitable for a dime novel. The credibility of his story is best judged in light of the compassion illustrated by a letter appearing in the ledger of the Eighty-third Pennsylvania:

Headquarters, 83rd Penna. Vols.
3rd Brigade, Porter's Division. Feb. 3rd 1862.
Brig. Gen'l Butterfield
Comr. of 3rd Brigade
Sir,
     I desire to call your attention to the case of Privates E.P. Bly of Co. C & R.A. Harvey of Co. A of this Regt.
     The first of these men was confined in the Guard House on the 10th, and the last on the 29th, of November last -- both under the charge of "disobedience"--- They were soon afterward tried by a General Court Martial, of which Col. Lansing 17th N. Y. Vols, was President.   Their sentences have never been promulgated. For nearly three months, these men have _____ in the Guard House exposed to the cold and dampness of an inclement winter --- Harvey is seriously injured by this treatment. I request very respectfully therefore this matter be brought to the attention of the proper authority.

Your Obt. Servant,
Strong Vincent
Lieut. Col. 83rd Regt. Pa. Vols.

APPENDIX IV
Norton on Little Round Top

Numerous theories have worked their way into the history books with regard to the events leading up to Vincent's occupation of Little Round Top, most of them crediting Generals Warren, Sykes, or Barnes, or any combination of the three. A host of reputable historians have provided a fascinating plethora of speculation. William Swinton, General Abner Doubleday, General Francis A. Walker, General Henry A. Hunt, and General Regis de Trobriand all contend in their works that Warren, on his own authority, detached Vincent to defend Little Round Top. The Comte de Paris mentions that General Sykes ordered Vincent's occupation. Lieutenant Colonel William H. Powell and J.H. Stine assert that Warren was responsible, but that the Sykes-Barnes chain of command was followed.

The Official Reports of General Sykes and Barnes do not provide particularly enlightening accounts either: Sykes says Warren posted the brigade, and Barnes maintains that he himself ordered Vincent's placement at Sykes' direction.

In *The Attack and Defense of Little Round Top*, Oliver Norton dismisses all of these versions, and others. Swinton "has confused the time and order of events and the movements of troops," and Norton cites the authoritative post-war correspondence of Warren, Roebling, and Mackenzie.

Doubleday's version, says Norton, is "imaginary.... Doubleday may have been well informed about the first day's battle, but he makes no claim to have been with the troops on the left..., and apparently got his information of what took place there, at least to some extent, from rumors...."

Norton says "One wonders where General Walker obtained [his] information about Warren detaching Vincent's brigade. He certainly did not get it from Warren....Warren's statements in his own letters show that....Walker is mistaken."

Hunt's account, including the sequence of events, is tersely dismissed. Norton simply says Hunt is mistaken, owing to his position as artillery commander, which gave him no connection to infantry movements.

Norton derogates de Trobriand's version as "another example of erroneous statements by a writer who was not present."

Norton has high praise for the accuracy of most of Comte de Paris' narration, but disputes several details including the contention that Sykes positioned Vincent.

Although numerous elements in Powell's description are criticized by Norton, he says "I can forgive him in consideration of his splendid tribute to the gallantry of Vincent's brigade...."

Stines' account, says Norton, contains "some statements not corroborated by any evidence," including his assertion that Warren approached Sykes and Barnes to request placement of Vincent.

Norton believes "Barnes' statement in his official report, that Warren in person came to Sykes is pure fiction."

Finally, in a letter written nine years after the battle to Captain Porter Farley of the 140th New York, General Sykes says, "How Vincent got to Round Top I do not know, unless hearing my aide-de-camp deliver the order for the Corps to take the left of the line, he made his way there of his own soldierly instinct."

No one was in a better position than Oliver Willcox Norton himself to witness the events which culminated in the timely occupation of Little Round Top. He explains his unique advantage: "Although a private soldier, I was at the time of the battle of Gettysburg, and for some time before and after, on detached service at the Headquarters of the Third Brigade..., commanded when the battle began by Colonel Strong Vincent. I was brigade bugler, mounted, and bearer of the brigade headquarters flag. As such, it was my duty to keep near the brigade commander, following him closely wherever he went, when the army was on the march or moving about a battlefield.... This duty gave me a better opportunity than even the officers of the brigade staff enjoyed, to see what occurred and hear verbal orders given or received.... I remained constantly with the brigade commander."

In November of 1863, Oliver Norton received a commission as a First Lieutenant in the 8th U.S. Colored Infantry. After his discharge at war's end, he joined his brother in an extremely successful business venture that would eventually spawn the American Can Company. In 1870 he married Lucy Colt Fanning, with whom he would have five children. He was troubled by progressively failing eyesight until his blindness became nearly total in 1894.

Source
Norton, O.W., *The Attack and Defense of Little Round Top.*

APPENDIX V
"Don't Yield An Inch."

The following verse, written by a poet identified only as "L.C.R.", is rife with poetic license. The piece appeared in the Thursday, July 23, 1863 edition of the *Erie Weekly Gazette*.

"The voice of Col. VINCENT rang clear above the din and preparation and the tramp, tramp, tramp of the advancing army. "Don't yield an inch, boys," were his words. He jumped upon a rock, waved his sword, and at that moment received a ball."--*Cor. Boston Journal.*

"DON'T YIELD AN INCH, BOYS"

Vaulting from his saddle to a rocky height,
Waving high his glittering sword above his bright young
head.
With foot firm planted toward the foe,
With lip of steel and eye of fire,
His clarion voice rang loud and clear

Along the serried ranks --
"Don't yield an inch, boys! don't yield an inch!"
But late beneath the classic elms of Yale
That youthful hero strolled;
War then to him was but an idle tale--
A tale by Grecian Poets told.
But when the blazing brand
Was hurled by fiendish hand
Across our peaceful land,
The volume then he cast aside.
With strong right arm the sword he drew
From out its scabbard yet unstained,
And to the battle field he flew.
Foremost in every conflict fierce
His youthful form was seen;
His valor and his knightly grace
Of every tongue the theme

But when upon that fatal Rock
He sprang, with one mad bound.
Then, met he war's relentless shock!
There, Immortality he found!

Let bleeding Love her solace find.
In that her Idol is enshrined
Within our heart of hearts,
That he, the Scholar ripe, the Soldier brave,
The Patriot pure, the Christian true,
Shall never age nor sorrow know.

No chance can dim his garlands fair;
No time can touch his clustering hair;
But ever in immortal youth,

In Love, Fidelity and Truth,
Upon that monumental Rock,
VINCENT the Brave through time shall stand!
And on that rock inscribed shall be,
In letters bright
With living light,
"Vivere Sat Vincere!"

L.C.R.

Five months after the battle, John P. Vincent, an Erie judge and second cousin of Strong, responded to a request for details from a Gettysburg lawyer.

Erie, Pa.
Nov. 30th 1863
D. McConaughy Esq.

Dear Sir,

Your favor of the 23rd inst. came to hand on Saturday too late for attention in that day. It gives me much pleasure to comply with your request for some of the particulars attending the wounding & death of Genl. Vincent.

He commanded the 3rd Brigade 1st Div. 5th Army Corps. This Corps arrived on the ground near the left of our Army in the morning of the 2nd of July about 2 o'clock. Gen. Vincent and his aide snatched a little repose on a garden gate torn from its hinges. Early in the forenoon his Brigade was ordered to hold the extreme left of our position near Little Round Top. He got into position in time to help Gen. Sykes repulse the first attempt to turn our flank.

Early in the afternoon a large body of the enemy made a desperate attempt to break our line, and it was at this time that he received his wound. He had gone into the battle in such a hurry that he had not time to unstrap his sword from his horse, and his only weapon was his heavy riding whip, but as many men in his Brigade knew him he needed no special insignia of office. It is related that seeing one of his men as he supposed skulking he used his whip freely over his shoulders as he drove him back into the ranks. Seeing the formidable numbers of the enemy compared with his own Brigade he sprang upon a rock and shouted in his clear ringing voice, "Don't give an inch boys" "don't give an inch" and while standing thus exposed and thus encouraging his men by voice and example he received a bullet through hip and groin, which caused his death on the 4th day afterwards.

He was at once carried to a farm house in the rear of our lines where all that could be done was done for him, but the surgeon at once pronounced the wound mortal.

He bore his sufferings with the patient endurance of a christian soldier and during the whole time though the wound must have been excruciatingly plainful, not a murmur or a groan was heard from him.

For a few hours before his death he was unconcious [*sic*]. & his last concious [*sic*] word was the repetition of the Lords prayer.

He fell a martyr to duty. He exposed himself with much rashness in the battlefield, but did so because he thought such an example necessary to his men to keep them up to the point of resistance necessary to hold the position which he knew must be held at whatever sacrifice.

He was young, -- but 26 years of age & left as bright professional prospects as were before any young man in the Country when he entered the army.   He entered in the first regt. of 3 mos. men as a private. Was soon elected Lieut. then appointed adjutant. He performed the duties of that office so acceptably that when his old Col. raised a regt., the 83rd Pa. for the war he was unanimously elected Lieut. Col. and on the death of Col. McLane was with equal unanimity elected Colonel & was then promoted to the Command of the Brigade to which his regt. was attached.   He fell near to Little Round Top - - it must have been near the center of the extreme left Brigade which as I learn rested on Round Top, and a little to its rear as our army faced.   Perhaps I have wearied you with details that are useless to you, but I hope you can cull from them what you want.

I would suggest the following as names for local committee in regard to battlefield matter.

Prescott Metcalf

John Clemens

A.H. Caughey

J.W. Douglass

M. Hartleb

W.S. Brown

Erie, Pa.

Do you want local committees for other places in the Co.

with much Respect

Yr. obt. Servt.

Jno. P. Vincent

APPENDIX VI
Where Did Vincent Fall?

Owing primarily to mistakes and misunderstandings made by veterans of the battle, the exact position where Colonel Vincent was standing when he was mortally wounded has been the subject of debate for many years.

Two conflicting markers bear witness to the controversy. The appearance of the first was noted as early as October 1864 by Issac Morehead, an Erie journalist touring the battlefield. 1 It was anonymously carved into a boulder near where today stands the Forty-fourth New York monument:

COL. STRONG VINCENT FELL HERE
COM 3RD. BRIG. 1ST DIV. 5 CORPS
JULY 2ND 1863

In what may be an indication of an amateur hand, the letter *S* carved in "1ST" and "CORPS" is backwards.

The 44th New York monument on Little Round Top, circa 1930. Vincent may have stood upon the group of boulders to the right while trying to rally the 16th Michigan.

The carved inscription on Vincent's rock.

The second marker is a marble slab mounted on a rock farther down the slope toward the Eighty-third Pennsylvania monument. Erected by the Erie G. A. R. Strong Vincent Post 67 in 1878, this was the first permanent marker on the Gettysburg battlefield outside of the National Cemetery. The top of the cenotaph is in the shape of a Maltese cross, across which is written:

3D BRIGADE
FIRST DIVISION
5TH CORPS

The area bellow the cross is inscribed:

GEN. STRONG VINCENT
WOUNDED
JULY 2, DIED JULY
7, 1863

Whether by design or omission, the inscription does not specifically say this was the location of Vincent's wounding -- only that he was, in fact, wounded.

The 1878 marker was authorized by a G.A.R. committee including Eighty-third's Captain John Graham of Company C. At a veterans' ceremony on Little Round Top, the carving on the boulder was noted, but "every one of the 83rd regiment were of the opinion that this was an erroneous location." [2]

In 1911 Oliver Norton was asked to join another committee being formed to definitely establish the site, as the two conflicting monuments had been the cause of "unpleasant remarks." In a letter to Captain M.V.B. Gifford of the committee, Norton declined the invitation, citing two reasons: "In the first place, while I was very near the spot I did not see Col. Vincent when

(Top)The present-day cenotaph
on Little Round Top.
(Lower right) The original marker,
damaged in the 1960's.

he fell. In the second place, if I should go to Gettysburg with the committee and attempt to locate the spot, I could be of no assistance on account of my blindness. I would be very apt to make a mistake about it." Norton's reply went on to disparage the marble cenotaph: "In my opinion this inscription is clearly wrong. That rock afforded a good view of all the regiments of the brigade and I think Vincent stood there from the time the brigade got into place until the break occurred in the 16th Michigan, when he went there to stop it." 3

Writing in 1865, Captain Amos Judson, Company E, Eighty-third Pennsylvania, refers to the locations in close agreement to Norton's version. He says Vincent "mounted a rock that he might overlook and direct the operations of the impending battle.... The Sixteenth...became somewhat thrown into confusion and a portion of them ran to the rear.... Seeing the danger Col. Vincent descended from the rock... [and] drove the men to the front..."4

Unfortunately, most of the actual eyewitnesses to the wounding of Vincent were members of the retreating Sixteenth Michigan, who would be understandably reluctant to write about it. However, Lieutentant Colonel Norval E. Welch's official report, while inaccurate and self-serving, contains an interesting detail which may lend additional credence to the Norton and Judson accounts. Welch said that "someone (supposed to be General Weed or Major General Sykes) called from the extreme crest of the hill to fall back..." 5 Perhaps, in the smoke and din of battle, Colonel Vincent's entreaty to "go back" was confused for a general's order to "fall back."

The Norton description, expanded on by him in a letter to Colonel Vincent's brother in 1914, would seem to be the most logical scenario. Vincent made his brigade headquarters at the boulder which now contains the marble cenotaph, as this location, especially if one stands on the rock, affords a view

which extends almost to both ends of the brigade line.   When
he saw the Sixteenth Michigan falling back across the rear of the
Forty-fourth New York, he ran up the slope to rally them.
Perhaps, although not specifically mentioned by Norton, he then
climbed atop the boulder which today contains the inscription,
in an attempt to be seen and obeyed more readily in the mass
confusion of the retreat.   After being shot, he was returned to
the relative security of the first boulder, where he remained until
the firing had subsided.   It is quite possible that the veterans who
located this as the site of the wounding did so because they saw
him there after he had been shot, assuming this was the place it
had happened.4

Sources

1.   Moorhead, Issac.   The Occasional Writings of Issac
Moorehead, With a Sketch of His Life. A.H. Caughey, Erie,
Pennsylvania, 1882. Reprinted in "The American Magazine and
Hsitorical Chronicle."   Volume 1, Number 2, Autumn-Winter
1985-86.   Clements Library, University of Michigan, Ann
Arbor, Michigan. Pp. 24-25.
2.   "Star & Sentinel."   August 1, 1878.   Quoted in letter dated
October 20, 1993 to Myra Wright from John S. Heiser, Facility
Management Specialist, National Park Service, Gettysburg.
3.   Letter dated August 13, 1911 to Captain M.V.P. Gifford from
O.W. Norton.   Reprinted in *Army Letters*.   Page 373.
4.   Judson. Pp. 126-128.
5.   Welch's Official Report.
6.   Letter dated August 3, 1914 to Bishop Boyd Vincent from
O.W. Norton.   Reprinted in *Army Letters*.   Pp. 386-387.

Appendix VII
Where Did Vincent Die?

For years researchers have been hard-pressed to say that Strong Vincent died, as a matter of absolute fact, in the Lewis A. Bushman farmhouse. The 19th Century structure was torn down just after the war and replaced, several hundred feet distant, with a brick house. Nearby is a frame house, called "Diener" on the Comte de Paris' map, which apparently was rented to tenant farmers near the Bushman property.

In 1888, Oliver Norton referred to the Comte de Paris' landmarks when writing an article for an encyclopedia entry about the battle. Speaking of the wounded Vincent, he said "...he was carried off to a farm house some mile or more in the rear. I should think it might be the house marked on the Comte de Paris' map Diener, on the road running southeast from Little Round Top."

In 1913, when Norton published *Attack and Defense of Little Round Top*, he wrote that after the battle he "saw Colonel Welsh sitting on his horse near the Bushman house.... Welsh told me that Colonel Vincent was in that house. This was the Bushman that Colonel Vincent was in that house. This was the Bushman farm house, where Vincent had been carried after receiving his fatal wound."

Captain Amos Judson, in his 1865 *History of the Eighty-Third Regiment Pennsylvania Volunteers*, said, "Colonel Vincent was carried to the farm house of Mr. Wm. Bushman, about two miles from Round Top...." Research indicates there was no *William* Bushman farm, but there was a George Bushman farm, which was used as a field hospital by the Twelfth Corps.

To complicate the issue even further, A. Pierson Case wrote his "Notes on the Taking and Holding of Little Round Top at Gettysburg" in 1866, in which he said:

> The Fifth Corps hospital had been made at the house and barns of J. Weikert on the Taneytown (Rd)... and during this cannonade (July 3, afternoon) many of the rebel shells came over the hill and struck our hospital, wounding some a second time. It was then moved to Lewis Bushman's, about a mile to the southeast.

Dr. Clinton Wagner, Chief Surgeon of the Fifth Corps' Second Division, wrote in 1911 that he selected the Jacob Weikert house as a field hospital on July 2nd, and he continued to perform operations there until about nine o'clock in the morning of July 3rd, when all the wounded were moved to a safer location. He also recalled seeing in the house the bodies of those three magnificent warriors shot at about the same time and place as Vincent: Colonel O'Rorke, General Weed, and Lieutenant Hazlitt.

If Case's and Wagner's memories were correct, how did Norton and others locate Vincent in the Bushman house on the evening of July 2nd?

Most likely, Vincent was first brought to the Jacob Weikert

rear of Little Round Top.   It may have been so over-crowded with wounded by that time that it was necessary to soon relocate Vincent and others to the Lewis Bushman house a mile farther to the rear.   Both hospitals would then have been operating simultaneously, until the relative security of the Weikert farm became threatened to a degree sufficient to make prudent the relocation of the remaining patients to the Bushman property.

Almost three months after the battle, on September 29, 1863, a son was born to Mr. & Mrs. Lewis Bushman. He was named Strong Vincent Bushman in memory of the fallen hero who died in their home.   Lizzie heard of this honor and sent the Bushmans a fine cut-glass pitcher as a gift.   Strong Vincent Bushman died in Hanover in 1937 and is buried in Evergreen Cemetery in Gettysburg.

Sources

Coco, G., *A Vast Sea of Misery*.
Norton, O.W., *The Attack and Defense of Little Round Top*.
Judson. Amos, *History of the Eighty-Third Regiment*.
Novotny, Debra, "Strong Vincent's Namesake." The Battlefield Dispatch, Oct. 1995, p. 2.

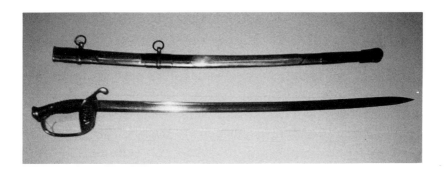

Appendix VIII
The Sword of Strong Vincent.

    Elizabeth Vincent presented her husband's sword, which had been left strapped to Vincent's saddle during his last battle, to Oliver Norton's son, Strong Vincent Norton, complete with a small brass presentation plate affixed to the scabbard. Perhaps as young Norton grew increasingly weary of standing in the shadow of a dead soldier, a rift began to develop between the Nortons that would seperate them for years to come.

    In December 1912, the elder Norton wrote to the General's brother Boyd, an Episcopal bishop and Lizzie's host, sponsor, and benefactor. Now seventy-three and in failing health, Norton asked the Bishop's advice on what to do with the sword: "I have always been sorry that I permitted her to leave it to my son who proved unworthy of it, but although his name was put on it, the sword has never left my possession. He has renounced all desire to have it and has even talked of changing his name. The plate could easily be removed and another one substituted."

    The letter goes on to suggest that the sword be sent to the National Museum of Washington, where it could be seen "by many people who now know and reverence his name and others who will come after them.... It really seems to me it ought to belong to the nation which he gave his life to save."1

Bishop Vincent concurred, and spoke with Lizzie about Norton's suggestion. She consented, and Norton began making arrangements with the museum, including a condition that the sword would be permanently displayed. Norton also insisted on replacing the presentation plate to his son with another to the museum. 2

Long since removed from "permanent" display, the sword resides today in a climate-controlled weapons vault at the Smithsonian Institution's National Museum of American History, catalog number 14438, acquisition number 55740.

As 19th Century weaponry goes, it is of suprisingly simple design, similar to that carried by lower-ranking officers. One side of the ricasso is inscribed "W.H. Horstmann & Son Philadelphia," and the reverse bears the words "Iron Proof." Two plates adorn the scabbard. The first is engraved: "Presented to the National Museum, Washington, D.C. By Elizabeth Carter Vincent Widow of Strong Vincent 1913." The second is marked: "Sword of Strong Vincent, Brigadier General U.S. Volunteers. This sword was carried by Strong Vincent, from April, 1861 to July 2, 1863, as Adjt. Three Months Volunteers, Lieut. Col. and Colonel Eighty-third Regiment Pennsylvania Volunteers Commanding Third Brigade, First Division, Fifth Army Corps at Little Round Top, Gettysburg, Mortally wounded July 2, died at Gettysburg July 7, 1863."

Norton died in 1920 at the age of 81. Lizzie predeceased him in 1914 at 76. Soon after her death, Norton wrote to Bishop Vincent: "You and I loved her.... As I look back over it I can recollect nothing which has given me greater pleasure outside of family matters than what I have been able to do for the memory of our war hero and those that were so dear to him. She was a noble woman, and her life was filled with joy and suffering.

Her memory will be dear to me as long as I can recollect anything...."3

Lizzie's final remembrance of Norton was in Item IX of her Last Will and Testament: "To Oliver W. Norton, to be expended for the best cigars he can buy, I give and bequeath the sum of Two Hundred and Fifty ($250.00) Dollars."4

Sources

1.   Letter from O.W. Norton to Bishop Boyd Vincent dated December 31, 1912. Copy in the author's collection. Original in the Clarke Historical Library, Central Michigan University.
2.   Letter from O.W. Norton to R. Rathbun, Assistant Secretary of the National Museum dated January 24, 1913, and
    Letter from O.W. Norton to Mrs. Elizabeth Vincent dated January 27, 1913, and
    Letter from Mrs. Elizabeth Vincent to R. Rathbum dated January 28, 1913, and
    Letter from O.W. Norton to Mrs. Strong Vincent dated February 5, 1913, and
    Letter from O.W. Norton to Mrs. Vincent dated February 11, 1913.
...All from the Clark Historical Library and marked as above. Copies in the author's collection.
3.   Norton, *Army Letters*, p. 365.
4.   Ibid. p. 362-363.

APPENDIX IX
A Final Tribute.

Perhaps the most stirring tribute to Strong Vincent came from Captain Amos Judson, who in writing his *History of the Eighty-third Regiment Pennsylvania Volunteers 1861-1865*, spoke of his commander and friend:

> Of his character as a man, and a soldier, it is unnecessary for me to speak in any terms of eulogy or admiration, for his fame is more widely known already than this book will ever be, and his name will be remembered when these pages shall have passed into oblivion. I have no practice in the language of econium, and I am not aware that my humor ever ran in that direction. But there have lived and died men of such stamp as must extort praise from even the most critical. When the regiment first went out, his style, as it was called, was not much admired by the men. But when they came to learn that his bearing was the result not of superciliousness, but of a noble dignity of character, they fell into an admiration of him, and this admiration grew and expanded day by day. And when they came to witness his skill in handling the regiment, and the brigade,

on the field of battle, and how he fought side by side, and shared all the dangers equally with them, the seal of his superiority became stamped upon their hearts. He had none of the tender regard for the safety of his own person when the occasion called for his services at the front, which I have seen some general officers manifest; none of that cunning strategy that would sneak for shelter behind a rock, a quarter of a mile to the rear, under the plea that the life of a commanding officer was of more importance than the lives of his men; none of that love of life, that would ask others to go where he dared not go himself. Yet his bravery had nothing of rashness in its composition. If he was always first and foremost on the field of battle it was because his sense of duty took him there, and if he became animated in the excitement of the fray, it was the result of a glorious enthusiasm which rose higher and higher as the joy of battle swelled in his breast and inspired him to dare and to do all that might become a man. In camp and in private life, his manners were those of a gentleman. He associated with the highest officers in the army, and I always noticed on such occasions that when in his company they behaved as if they felt themselves in the presence of a *Man*. But perhaps the greatest thing that can be said in his favor is that amidst all the unfavorable influences in the life of a soldier he never forgot the religous training he had received in his early years. I have frequently known him, after coming in from business at the front, at bed-time, to put out the light and kneel by his little cot and spend a few moments in silent prayer before retiring to rest. But I have done with what some may deem the language of adulation. Personally I am not a professed admirer of any man, living or dead; but I cannot let this opportunity pass without giving the result of my observations on the character of one with whom I have been associated in arms. To sum up the character of Gen. Strong Vincent in three words, I can only say that he was a gallant soldier, a fine scholar and a Christian gentleman, and when you say this you have said all that can be said of any man.

The gravemarker of General Strong Vincent.

**(Top) Gravemarker of Elizabeth Vincent,
(Bottom) Blanche Strong Vincent.**

APPENDIX X
Letters & Orders

The following letters and orders taken from regimental and brigade ledgers provide an interesting overview of Strong Vincent's military life.

Head Quarters 83rd Penna. Vols.
Camp Near Sharpsburg, Md.
Oct. 14th 1862.

Lieut. J. H. Barnet
    Lieutenant,
    I am directed to inform you that in consequence of your protracted inability for duty by reason of Sickness, and in view of the pressing necessity of the service for officers.   Your resignation will probably be promptly accepted.
    You are therefore requested to forward the same within two days from this date.

                        By Command of
                        Col. Strong Vincent

Head Quarters 83rd Penna. Vols. 3rd Brigade
Butterfield's Div. Porter's Corps.
Nov. 1st 1862.

Lt. Lansing, ΛΛΛG,
Lieutenant,
    In obedience to special order 301.-- Headquarters Army of
the Potomac. I respectfully designate:
        Capt. D.C. McCoy Co. F.
        Sergt. Robt. Gilmore Co. D.
        Sergt. M.E. Halderman Co. K.
as competent officers to take charge of and conduct drafted men
to this regiment.
    I would also request that permission be given to the party
to proceed to Pittsburg instead of Harrisburg, as the drafted men
from the county in which the Regt. was raised are in rendezvous
at the former place, and can be easily secured.
    I would respectfully suggest also, in view of the large
number of men required to fill the Regt. to the maximum (280)
that two additional Commissioned and eight Non-Commissioned
Officers be detailed for the duty named. In case permission is
given for a further detail I would suggest the following additional
names --

Capt. John M. Sell Co. I.   Lt. M.V. Gifford Co. A.
Corp. C.W. Hubbell Co. I.   Sergt M. Howard Co. A.
Sergt. W. McCracklin Co. B.   Sergt. I. Moore Co. D.
Sergt. B.B. Hyne Co. H.   Sergt. L. Burford Co. G.

                          Your Obt. Servant,
                          Strong Vincent
                          Col. 83rd Penna. Vols.

Head Quarters 83rd Penna. Vols. 3rd Brigade
Butterfield's Div. Porter's Corps.
Nov. 1st 1862.
Lt. Lansing A.A.AG.
Lieutenant,
   In compliance with Circular from Head Quarters Butterfield's Div., I have to report that Two Hundred and Eighty (280) men are required to fill this regt. to the maximum. That Two Hundred and Eighty stand of arms and Two Hundred and Eighty sets of Equipments are also required.

> 280 men
> 280 Springfield Rifle, Cal. 58.
> 280 Sets equipments.

> > Your obt. Servant
> > Strong Vincent
> > Col. 83rd Penna. Vols.

Head Quarters 83rd Penna.
3rd Brigade 1st Div. 5th Army Corps.
Nov. 21st 1862.
Colonel Pulston
Mil. Ajt. Penna.
Colonel,
   I remember that you were concerned one year ago in the presentation by Senator Cowan, on the part of the State of Penna., of elegant national flag to this regt. We have born it through half a score of battles, amid the storm and sun of the Peninsular and Maryland Campaign, not without honor, nor without profit to our Country. The remnant which is left of it, tattered silk and

shivered lance proclaim the service it has seen, and reminds me daily that if we would have a vestige of it saved to hang in the halls of the State, it must have a successor soon.

Will you therefore be kind enough to cause a new one to be prepared and sent to us as soon as practable. Desiring to hear from you regarding this request

> I remain
> Your obt. servt.
> Strong Vincent
> Col. 83rd Penna. Vol.

Head Quarters 83rd Penna Vols.
Nov. 28th 1862
Surgeon Genl. King
Pittsburg, Penna

I have the honor to forward here with a return of the medical officers who have attached to this Command since its organization.

You will perceive that the position of Major Surgeon is vacant. I have declined to recommend either of the Asst. Surgeons present because I am of opinion that more competent medical men are to be had in the state, and it is of course desirable that the position should be filled by a superior man.

Will you not therefore take the earliest opportunity of selecting and attaching to this regt. a surgeon who will creditably represent alike this Command, his profession, and our State.

> Your obt. Servant
> Strong Vincent
> Col. 83rd Penna.

Head Quarters
83rd Regt. Penna. Vols.
Nov. 28th, 1862.

Genl. S. Thomas
Adjt. Genl. U.S. Army
Washington, D.C.

General,

I have just recd. a copy of an extract from Special Order No. 359 War Dept A.G.O. Nov. 22nd/62 in which it is directed that Surgeon Wm. Faulkner 83rd Penna. Vols. be dropped from the rolls for absence without leave.

I have the honor to call the attention of the Dept. of Special Order No. 281 H.Q. Army of the Potomac Oct. 14th 1862 by which the same officer (among others) having tendered his resignation is honorably discharged from the Service.

A revocation of so much of the former order as applies to him will protect the reputation of a most accomplished Surgeon whose sight has been sacrificed while in the performance of his duty upon the field.

I have the honor to be
Your Obt. Servt.
Strong Vincent
Col. 83rd. Penna. Vols.

Head Quarters 83rd Penna. Vols.
Dec. 26th 1862.
Hon. Saml. B. Thomas
Dept. Sec. Com. Penna.

Sir,

I have the honor to acknowledge the receipt of yours of the 23rd, enclosing commissions.   Lt. [James M.] Hunter is discharged by reason of disability, the commission however will be sent him.   Lt. [John] Harrington fell at Bull Run.   His commission I will forward to his parents.

I addressed the Adjt. Genl. a few days since, asking the Governor to appoint and commission a number of officers who have won promotion by gallantry and attention to duty. Among them some who are enclosed in your communications, that list is correct and complete up to date.

Be kind enough to call the notice of the Governor to the claim of these young men, and assure him of the continued devotion of the regiment to the old state and our good cause.

Your Obt. Servant
Strong Vincent
Col. 83rd Penna. Vols.

Head Quarters 83rd Penna. Vols.
January 7th 1863.
Dr. James King, Surgeon Genl. Penna.
Sir,

I had the honor to receive your communication of the 13th ult. informing me of the appointment of Asst. Surgeon E. P. Allen of the 141st Penna. to the Regt. and also that A. Surgeon Walborne of the 83rd was to be transferred to the 17th Penna. Cavalry.

At the close of the letter, to which yours of the 13th is an answer you will observe I inquired as to the capacity and qualifications of Surgeon Church of the 141st Penna, adding that he might be assigned if competent; in as much as he deserved to be relieved from that Regt. in order to make way for Dr. Allen's promotion to a Maj. Surgeon therein, who it seems is the choice of that Regt. as was the family physician of many of its officers and men. It occurs to me that you may have misunderstood my communication so far as to have confused the names of these two gentlemen; Dr. Church having been asked for & Dr. Allen sent.

If such is the case, I would be oblidged to you if you will recall the former assignment and thus please both parties and advance the interest of the service.

If authority to transfer is beyond the power of the Med. Dept. of the State I should be pleased to accompany my application to the War Dept. with an approbutory letter from yourself.

I trust the transfer of Dr. Walborne will be permanent.
I have the honor to remain,

Your Obt. Servt.
Strong Vincent
Col. 83rd Penna.

Head Qrs. 83rd Penna. Vols.
3rd Brig. 1st Div. 5th Army Corps
Jan. 10th 1863.

Capt. Estes
A.A.A.Genl.

Captain,

I have the honor to ask from the War Dept., through the proper channels, the transfer of Surgeon Wm. Church of the 141st Penna. to the Surgeonship of this regt. and the appointment of Surgeon E.P. Allen who has lately been directed to report to the latter Regiment, but has not yet been mustered to the same position in the former.

My reason for the request and circumstances are as follows: Drs. Church and Allen have both for sometime been assigned for duty to the 141st Penna. the first as Maj. Surgeon, the second as an Asst.   Dr. Allen who is a man of middle age, of skill and experience, was at home the family physician of many of the officers and men -- was promised by the Governor of Penna. a full Surgeoncy and expected it in that Regt. -- Dr. Church, a very young man, a stranger to the regt. was assigned as Surgeon over him -- Dr. Church regarding the preference of the regiment and the just expectation of Dr. Allen, asked to be transferred to the 83rd Pa. where he is known, and in which the position of Surgeon was vacant.   The same request was also made by the Surgeon Genl. of Pa. by myself. Evidently misunderstanding the request he replied he had assigned Dr. Allen with rank of Surgeon to this regiment.

In order to secure the better satisfaction of all parties and thus

advance the interests of the regt. and of the service -- I must respectfully ask that Surgeon Church be transferred to the 83rd Penna. and Surgeon Allen assigned to the 141st Penna.
I am, Sir, Very respectfully

> Your obt. Servt.
> Strong Vincent
> Col. 83rd Penna.

Head Qrs. 83rd Pa. Vols.
Jan. 14th 1863

General:

Presuming that a note will trouble you less than a personal interview, I send it instead. You will doubtless remember the subject of our conversation yesterday concerning the resignation of one of my officers, Capt. [Phineas P.] Carpenter seemed highly gratified with the terms you offer, but after considering it carefully tells me, he believes it to be his duty clearly to leave the service if his superiors will permit: -- that while a leave of absence for twenty or thirty days would perhaps suffice to arrange his business partly, yet it could not take the responsibility of his wife, who, I am convinced is an invalid and dependant ever upon his return for her life. Rather, therefore than tender his resignation again at the experation of his leave, he asks to go now.

Capt. Carpenter is an excellent officer. He has been throughout the campaigns of nearly two years. No man of this regt. ever questioned his bravery. I should be sorry to lose him but I believe as strong a sense of duty impels him to leave the service as first induced him to enter it.

I would therefore respectfully ask, Genl. that so much of the order discharging him as refers to the manner in which the resignation is supposed to be tendered, be recalled and that he be <u>honorably</u> discharged from the service.
I am, General,

>Your Obt. Servt.
>Strong Vincent
>Col. 83rd P.V.
>Maj. Genl. Hooker
>Comdg. Army of the Potomac.

Head Quarters 83rd Penna.
January 26th 1863.
Capt. J.P. Sherborne
A.A.Genl.

Captain,
    Yours of the 14th is received informing of the failure of Lt. E.W. Reid of this regt. to report as directed at the Head Quarters of the Military Dis. of Washington.
    You will oblige me if it can be done, by arresting this officer again and causing him to be sent direct to Acquia Creek for his regt. Any means the General may accept of securing his return will be thankfully acknowledged by me.

>Your Obt. Servant
>Strong Vincent
>Col. 83rd Penna.

Head Quarters 83rd Pa. Vols.
March 11th 1863.
Capt. Estes
A.A.A.Genl.
Captain,
    I have the honor to report in compliance with Circular Hd. Qrs. 5th Army Corps March 10th 1863, that my command is completely equiped for service, with the exception of 41 Springfield rifles required for & 10 Slings long since required; that from five to eight days substance is consistantly kept on hand, ten days of grain, and from five to ten days forage -- according to the supply at Brigade Commissary & Qr. Mrs. -- that my transportation consists of four six mule teams, all of which are in good condition.
I am, Sir, Very Respectfully
                                            Your Obt. Servt.
                                            Strong Vincent
                                            Col. 83rd Penna.

Head Quarters 83rd Penna. Vols.
March 17th 1863.
Captain Estes
A.A.A.G.

Captain,
    In reply to a communication from Hd. Qrs. 3rd Brigade, signed by command of Col. Stockton, and directing an investigation of the facts stated in an "Extract" from the report of The Field Officer of the Day, concerning the Guard of this regiment, I have the honor to state that by my direction all sentinels upon the front,

rear and flanks of this reg't. have been withdrawn; that but three posts are established, one at my H. Qrs., one at the Commissarys tent and one at the Guard House over the prisoners; that the number and position of sentinels as suggested by Gen. Reg. concerning Police Guard cannot be maintained in a camp whose lines are so interfered with by the tents and teams of other regiments, as are those of my command; that the post sentinels who have nothing to do but patrol their beats and give people salutes, is making a farce of Guard Duty, and endangering the efficiency of men when they are placed in positions demanding vigilance. The system of passes and Provost Patrols is expected to correct the evil of men going out of camp without leave. Sentinels cannot do it, and to order it from them is to ask a thing impractible.

This therefore being left to the sound direction of the Commanding Officer of a regt. his action is properly conclusive. I have the honor to be, Sir,

> Your obdt. Servt.
> Strong Vincent
> Col. 83rd Penna.

Head Quarters 83rd Penna. Vols.
March 19th 1863
Mr. S. Purley
Washington, D.C.

Dear Sir,

In order to facilitate the efforts of those who are endeavoring to obtain the clothing & private effects of enlisted men of this Regt. which were stored in Georgetown D.C. in March and February of last year, I have determined to send you the order empowering you at any time, until further direction to the contrary, to draw upon Capt. Hartz or Col. Baker or such other Govt. official as my have charge of these packages, your order in favor of the party entitled to receive them for all effects belonging to a deceased or a discharged soldier of this Regt. which may be there stored. This order you will of course make known to the Govt. Agent & keep a file of your orders.

In haste, very truly your friend

Strong Vincent
Col. 83 Penna.

Head Quarters 83rd Penna.
March 21, 1863.

Captain,

I reforward the two enclosed sets of papers for discharge. The others which were returned the Reg. Surgeon carried to the Med. Director of Div. to ascertain what was required. Upon consultation the Med. Director declared the statements upon the papers sufficient and directed him to leave them. These were retained in order that the Commanders of the Co's might say -- as they have done and as was to be presumed from the fact that no disease was stated by them before -- that they are ignorant of the nature of the complaint, "Atrophy of the large Gluteus muscle of the left side, interfering the functions of the joint" -- is hardly a disease which a Commanding officer of a Co. could state to emit as a fact upon his own knowledge.

I make the explanation to show you that these emits an

intention on the part of the officers refered to, to omit or evade any part of their duty.

Very Respectfully
Strong Vincent
Col. 83rd Penna.

Head Qrs. 83rd Pa. Vols.
March 24th, 1863.

Dr. James King,

I have the honor to report to you the acceptance of the resignation of Surgeon E.P. Allen of this regiment on the 23rd inst. for the reason assigned of the approaching death of his wife. His resignation, regretted by me both in its self and for its cause, has left my command without appropriate medical attention.

Asst. Surgeon Michael Thompson is now in charge. He is exceedingly anxious to obtain my recomendation & that of the Medical Directors of the Div. & Corps to you for promotion, which both myself and those officers do not deem it our duty to the regt. to give. I would ask you therefore Dr. to select from among the number of those whom you know to be well qualified for the medical charge of a regt. another Surgeon & Asst. who will be as acceptable as was Dr. Allen.

I am, Sir, Very Truly & Respectfully

Your Obt. Servt.
Strong Vincent
Col. 83rd Pa.

Head Qrs. 83rd Pa. Vols.
March 24th 1863.
Capt. Estis, A.A.A.Genl.
Captain,
    I have the honor to ask that Private Norton of "K" Co. of this regt. now detailed as a Bugler at Brigade Hd. Qrs. may be ordered to return to his regt. I ask this because I have had but one Bugler for months on duty with the command.
    He has grown authoritative & much wind broken and is no longer fit to do what he attempts. As there are a number of Buglers in other regiments of the Brigade better than Norton, and who can be more easily spared. I respectfully submit that my request is not improper or unjust, that the detail for that duty be taken from another regiment.
I am Capt. Very respectfully
                    Your Obt. Servt.
                    Strong Vincent
                    Col. 83rd Pa..

Head Quarters 83rd Pa. Vol.
April 3rd 1863.
General Order
No. 3}
    The commanding officer regrets that he is compelled to call the attention of the officers of his command to certain practices which have of late been observed in the Regiment and which are highly prejudicial to good order and military discipline.
    Every commanding officer is expected to maintain in his intercourse with enlisted men such a destinction as is due to the difference in their military grade. The officers who fail to

observe and enact this respect, compromise his own influence &
the discipline of the service.

Every commissioned officer is expected, likewise, when on
duty, not fatigue, to wear his sword and proper uniform, also all
officers on duty will appear at dress parade.

By Command of,
Col. Strong Vincent

Head Quarters 83rd Pa. Vols.
April 6, 1863.
Special Orders
No. 13}

Corporal James Swails of "G" Company having been given
a Furlough of ten days to go to Lewiston in the State of Penna.
of which he availed himself upon the 16th of March last failed
to return and report himself until the 5th day of April instant. By
virtue of the Act of Congress impowering a properly appointed
Field Officer of a regiment to try and punish all cases under the
jurisdiction of a Regimental Court Martial and by virtue of
circular from Hd. Qrs. 5th Army Corps, appointing commanding
officers of Regiments as such authorized persons, the Col. directs
that 4th Corporal James Swails of "G" Company be reduced to
the ranks and forfeit to the Government all pay during his absence
without leave. This sentence is made thus lenient because there
is reason to believe that part of the unauthorized absence of the
accused was unavoidable.

The detention while on Furlough of one day each in the cases
of Private [Ervin] Black of Co. "K" and Private [James] Allen
of Co. "I" being compulsory no punishment will be awarded. In
the cases of Private [Peter] Bender of Co. "I" and [Isaac N.]
Vancamp of Co. "H" arrested for straggling from camp without
a pass, in violation of existing orders they will each forfeit to the

Government five dollars of their monthly pay for the present month and be placed first on the roster of their respective companies for guard duty for each alternate day for one week from this date.

By Command of
Col. Strong Vincent

Head Quarters 83rd Penna.
April 12th, 1863
Col. [Matthew] Quay
Mil. Agent Penna.
My dear Col.

I found on my recent return from a short leave your note saying that if I would forward our old state flag to your office you would have a duplicate set of colors sent me.

I was much pleased to see that the Legislature had (I presume in accordance to your request) voted both us and the 111th a new flag.

I regret however that you place as a condition of our receiving it that the old one should be returned. You can easily understand how great a pride both officers and men have grown to feel in the old color which has so often victoriously waved over them in the fiercest of the fight -- and I believe they all love it the more because it is so sadly faded and riddled and torn. They can not bear on a march or a parade of ceromony to have the old flag absent. A fresh, bright color assuming the place of the old one, makes them all look the men say, like a new regiment. This sensitiveness is an honorable and natural one and I feel disposed, if possible, to gratify and respect it.

I propose to you, therefore, Col. in view of this state of

BATTLE FLAG OF THE 83 P.V.
Of the 3.ª Brigade, 1.ᵗ Division, 5.ᵗʰ Corps, Army of Potomac.

Siege of   Yorktown, April 4.ᵗʰ to May 4.ᵗʰ 1862.
Battle of   Hanover Court House, May 27.ᵗʰ   ,,
   ,,   ,,   Gains' Mill.............June 27.ᵗʰ   ,,
   ,,   ,,   Malvern Hill............July 1.ˢᵗ   ,,
   ,,   ,,   Bull Run,..............Aug. 29.ᵗʰ   ,,
   ,,   ,,   Antetam................Sept. 17.ᵗʰ   ,,
   ,,   ,,   Fredericksburg,.........Dec 13.ᵗʰ   ,,
   ,,   ,,   Chancellorsville,.......May 1, 2, 3, 1863.
   ,,   ,,   Gettysburg,.............July 1, 2, 3.   ,,

Period pencil sketch of Color Sergeant Alexander Rogers and the original Battle Flag of the Eighty-third Pennsylvania.

feeling in the regiment, to send us the new color which we will carry side by side with the old -- treating the veteran tenderly, handling it with care, giving it to the breeze in every fight but only then, and at the expiration of our period of service to return it to the state with as many good fights well fought under it as it may be our fortune to encounter, and with increased honor on every fold to the noble old state whose elegant gift it originally was. Let me hear from you as soon as possible, if you conclude to send the new color, I will direct my Purveyor to call for it.

> Your Obdt. Servt.
> Strong Vincent
> Col. 83rd Penna.

Head Quarters 83rd Pa. Vols.
April 22nd 1863.
Mr. Frank Moore
Sir:

The prospecters & specimen pages of your new work were received some weeks ago, and with them a request that I would forward to you a sketch of the services of Wm. J. Wittich of this regt. who distinguished himself at Malvern Hill by the capture of a rebel flag -- I send you herewith a brief record, which, though hasty, I trust does full honor to the memory of that gallant young officer.

> I am, Sir, Very respectfully
> Yr. Obt. Servt.
> Strong Vincent
> Col. 83rd Pa.

Wittich, William John, 1st Lieutenant of "I" Co. 83rd Pa. Vols., was born in Erie, Penna. Nov. 4th 1837. He received an Academic education and subsequently devoted his attention to the profession of a painter.

At the beginning of the war he enlisted as a private in what was known as the "Erie Regiment", commanded by Col. John W. McLane, for three months.   When this regiment was reorganized for the war he entered it as 3rd Sergt. and by his uniform good conduct soon rose to be Orderly Sergeant of his company.

At the battle of Malvern Hill, his regiment, which during the day was occupied in supporting a battery, was at 5 in the afternoon ordered to the extreme front to assist in checking the attack of the enemy fast becoming furious. The solid columns of the rebels had approached to with a hundred yards of the regiment and the batteries in its rear where a terrible storm of grape and bullets broke their first line and drove scattered and straggling backwards upon the second. In their flight, they left a stand of colors. Young Wittich observed them, obtaining the permission of his Captain, he darted in front of the regiment, passed diagnally along its whole front from right to left, under an incessant fire from batteries and musketry of both sides, quietly laid his gun in a little hollow, advanced to the brow of the hillock where the rebels had broken, seized the flag almost from their very grasps, raised it over his head and walked deliberately back to his place in the ranks, unharmed by a hostile or friendly bullet. He was made a Lieutenant on the field for his gallantry. At the grand review of the Army on the 4th of July following, he was brought out at the head of his regiment, prostrate with fever and the trophy of his daring was ordered by his General of Brigade to be lashed to his ambulance.

This flag is now deposited at the War Department in Washington and bears inscribed upon it the name of its brave captor. He survived his sickness to fall at the Second battle of Bull Run. On the morning of the second day after the fight, his twin brother Sergt. in the same Co. who had been severely wounded, was attempting to drag himself from the field. He had not proceeded ten paces from the spot where he had laid for two nights and a day when he came upon the corpse of his brother, his feet upwards and his face to the foe. He covered him with his blanket and was left to an unknown burial as brave a soldier and as glorious a youth as this Rebellion has numbered among its victims.

Head Quarters 3rd Brigade 1st Div. 5th Corps
May 19th 1863.
Dr. James King
Surg. Genl. Penna.

Doctor,
I enclose to you a report of changes in the Med. Dept. of the 83rd Penna. You have doubtless recd. official notice from the Adjt. Genls.' office of the vacancies by this time, and the object of my communication is to ask you to assign to the regt. as speedily your engagments will allow. At least one Asst. Surgeon -- Dr. Horting who recently resigned, made quite a favorable impression upon me, and I was sorry his physical disability compelled him to leave the field.
I am, Doctor, Very Respectfully

Your Obedient Servant,
Strong Vincent
Col. 83rd Penna.
Comdg. Brig.

Head Quarters 3rd Brigade
1st Div. 5th Corps
May 20th 1863.
General Orders
No. 1}
    The command of the Brigade is hereby assumed by the undersigned.
    The following Officers are announced as upon the staff of the Col. Commanding, and as such are temporarily detached from their respective regiments.
1st Lieut. Jno. M. Clark, 83rd Penna. Act. Asst. Adjt. Genl.
Capt. A. M. Judson, 83rd Penna. Act. Aide-de-camp.
1st Lieut. W. Jewett, 16th Michigan. Act. Aide-de-camp.
2nd Lieut. [Frank] Kelly, 44th N.Y. Vols. Act. Aide-de-camp.
Capt. [Eugene S.] Nash, 44th N.Y. Vols. Act. Inspc. Genl.
1st Lieut. [Minor] Newell, 16th Michigan. Act. Brig. Qr. Master.

> Strong Vincent
> Col. 83rd Penna. Vols.
> Comd'g Brigade

Head Quarters 3rd Brigade 1st Div.
5th Army Corps
May 20th 1863.
General Orders
No. 2}
    I. The Regiments of this Brigade will be prepared to break camp tomorrow at 7 A.M. The "Color" will sound at that hour.
    A Staff Officer will be in waiting there at Hd. Qrs. to direct each regiment to its new Camping ground. The Brigade will then be encamped in line of battle, the 83rd Pa. Vols. on the right, 44th N.Y. Vols. on the left, the 20th Maine in th right center &

the the 16th Michigan Vols. on the left center.

A front of 400 feet and a depth of 120 paces is assigned to each regiment.

The front line of the mens tents will be (10) Ten paces in rear of the "Color" line. The rear line if the mens tents, 40 paces in rear of their front line. The rear line: The Kitchens 20 paces in rear of the line of mens tents. The front line of Officers tents: 20 paces in rear of the Kitchens.

The front line of Field and Staff tents 30 paces in rear of the Company Officers tents. The mens tents will be two files facing on the company streets. Allowing two (2) men to a tent, an interval of two (2) feet between each rank and each file of tents and a street of 30 feet in width.

The lines will be formed, arranged and marked for each regt. The mens sinks will be dug at least 100 paces in advance of the Color line. The Brigade and Regimental teams will be parked in rear of the Camp on ground designated by the Brigade Qr. Master.

II. The attention of Regimental Commanders is called to a communication of the Med. Director of this Army in General Orders No. 52 Hd. Qrs. A of P.

> By Command of
> Col. Strong Vincent
> Comdg. Brigade

Head Quarters Brigade
May 20, 1863.
General Orders
No. 3}

I. The hours of service and parade of ceremony will be the same throughout the Brigade.

II.   Each duty will be ordered by its proper call sounded by the Bugler at these Head Quarters, and the Call at its close will be immediately taken up and repeated by the Bugler at Regimental Head Qrs.

III.

Reville	5 o'clock	A.M.
Breakfast Call	5:30	"
Sick Call	6:00	"
Drill " (By Company)	6:30	"
Recall	8:00	"
Assembly of the Guard	8:30	"

(The proper Troops will be sounded by the Drums of the Guard before beating off)

Dinner Call	12	P.M.
Drill Call (By Regt. or Brig)	4	"
Recall	6	"
Assembly (for dress parade)	6:45	"
To the Colors	7:00	"

The proper "Retreat" will be sounded by the Drum Corp of each Regt. before beating off.

Tattoo	8:30	"
Extinguishing lights Taps on the drums	9:00	"

IV. Brigade drills will be had on Tuesday and Thursdays.

V.   Saturdays will be given to the men as heretofore for purpose of Bathing and Washing clothes.

VI.   The usual Sunday morning inspection will be by Regiment at 10 A.M.

VII. Guard will hereafter by mounted by Brigade acending to the form indicated in General Butterfield's "Standing Order" with each alteration as will be verbally communicated by the A.A.A.G.

The detail from each regt. will be 1 Commissioned officer,

1 Sergeant, 2 Corp. and 21 men.

VIII.   Dress Parade will on Sundays be held by Brigade according to form to be hereafter designated.

By Command of
Strong Vincent
Col. Comdg. Brig.

Head Quarters 3rd Brigade 1st Div. 5th Corps.
June 1st, 1863.
Captain,

I have the honor to report everything quiet along my lines. The patrols and scouts from Deep Run to U.S. Gold Works report practicable crossings for a number of men at almost any point between Richard's Ferry and Deep Run. A path has been cut close to the waters edge concealed, along which the scouts operate.   I have established several forts of observation at intermediate points.   This will, I believe, prevent any communications by citizens or any crossing in force here.

Head Quarters, 3rd Brig. 1st Div. 5th Corps.
Captain____AAG
June 4th, 1863.
Captain,

I send to you a copy of a memorandum of information taken by Col. Rice from two deserters who came into my lines this afternoon. Instead of ordering them to Div. Hd. Qrs. in order that much information as would be immediately valuable to you might have been obtained. He questioned them himself and then sent them direct to Gen. Meade.

I trust this mode of procedure during my absence along the lines may not have deprived the Genl. Comd'g. the Div. of such information as reports from other parts of the lines may have suggested in inquiry for.

The enclosed memorandum. Col. R. who I have sent for assures me contains everything they knew of importance.

I have to add they confirm my fears about the desertion of a man from our lines. Corp. H.L. Davenport, Co. A, 16th Mich. Vols. crossed over at Ballard Dam to the enemy's lines. These deserters say that he gave the entire force of the brigade, and the disposition to them, and correctly as they repeated the information. I have also to report the appearance of infantry in considerable force opposite Richards Ford and Deep Run, last night, where cavalry have been stationed heretofore. A Rebel rocket signal was observed at 9:30 o'clock P.M. last night opposite U.S. Ford. The enemy's posts and pickets are evidently stronger than our own there.

Your obdt. Servt.
Col. Strong Vincent.

Head Quarters, 3rd Brig. 1st Div. 5th Corps.
June 8, 1863. 4 P.M.
Capt.

This artillery alluded to last night has evidently been put in position at Kemper's Ford. It is so masked as to prevent my obtaining the no. of guns. I have returned from this point and observed an officer of rank with a large escort, and staff which were left at the edge of the woods, ride to the ford. I have

ascertained the force opposite me pretty nearly the Second S.C. Mounted Infantry, one Va. Regt. probably the ninth and one N.C. Regt. form the Brigade which is doing duty in this vicinity. I shall probably know through the plan which is now opperating successfully more definately as to their number and names. I am much in need of those orderlies.
I am Capt.

> Your Obdt. Servt.
> Col. Strong Vincent
> Comdg. Brig.

Head Quarters 3rd Brig. 1st Div. 5th Corps.
June 8th 1863. 8 P.M.
Capt.

In compliance with suggestions of the General Comdg. Division I have ordered the 44th N.Y. to report by daylight at Kempers Ford in the position occupied by the 83rd Penna.

Col. Rice as well as all the Regimental commanders are directed to exercise the most constant vigilance. I am satisfied through my experiment to-day that I obtained correct information as far as it goes regarding the force opposite me. I directed an officer in whose inteligence and confidence could be placed, to disguise himself in a private uniform put on the badge of the 11th Corps, take some sugar and coffee and a little salt, and put himself apart from the rest of the pickets in communication with the enemy. He pretended to be holding a forbidden communication with them, and had no sooner put himself in view than they recognized his badge and cried out "hallo you damned dutchman, when did your Corps come up here." He naturally got angry and sputtered in broken English that he was as good as any rebel over the dam. At length as their butts, he got into conversation, revealed the presence of the supposed Corps, bartered his little bag of coffee and ascertained that their regt. was the Second S.C. mounted infantry a statement confirmed by their relief coming down on horseback and the pickets appearing on post without sabers and with Springfield muskets and infantry cartridge boxes, that a Virginia Regt. probably the 9th and a N.C. Regt formed the rest of the Brigade that they are all in the vicinity.

Col. Strong Vincent, Cmdg. Brig.

Head Quarters, 3rd Brig. 1st Div. 5th Corps.
June 11, 1863. 1:30 P.M.
Capt.,

I have the honor to report the following information obtained an hour since by communications with a rebel picket -- a native of the State of Iowa, at Ellis Ford.

He says Genl. Lee received the force of "Jackson's old Command," day before yesterday which is some three miles below "Ellis' Ford" and another larger force at the same distance up the river. He says the pickets left on the 9th because they feared "Stoneman from their left and another force from their right would cut them off." They are the same regiments who were here before, one brigade up and down the river.

They say they don't know the result of the fight up the river, think they got badly beaten, and in hopes to corroborate this statement by the report of another man whom I have in communication at Kemper's Ford.

I am Capt.

Your Obt. Servt.
Strong Vincent
Comdg. Brigade.

Head Quarters 3rd Brigade, June 13th, 1863.
General Order No. 4}

The enemy is receiving valuable aid and comfort at the hands of many citizens residing in the vicinity of this command. To correct this practice it is ordered:

I.   That Guards to the number of at least three, be placed at all houses from Fields Ford on the right; to Ellis Ford on the left; between the Kelly's Ford Road and the river.

II.   That three guards be instructed to permit no member of the family residing there, or other persons whatsoever, to leave the enclosure about the house except upon the written pass of the Regt. Commander whose troops are on duty there. To permit no intercourse there between the citizens of different families except-- in the presence of the Guards: To allow no officer, soldier, or civilian to enter such house except -- with a pass signed by the Regt. Commander responsible for the protection, or at these Hd. Qrs. All those violating this order will be arrested and sent to these Head Quarters and the names of all officers without passes will be taken by the guards, and the officers directed to report in arrest to the commandants of their regiments.

III.   All enlisted men or civilians of either sex, black or white, who are found outside the limits of their Regts. or homes without a proper pass will at once be arrested and sent to these Head Quarters. A staff officer will designate the houses which are to be assigned to the supervision of each Regt. Commander. Constant vigilance is our best protection in an enemy's country against scouts, spies, and guerillas. The duty of every officer in the respect is manifest, and will be required of him.

By Command of
Strong Vincent
Col. Comdg. Brig.

Members of Vincent's Brigade gather on Little Round Top, during Remembrance Day Ceremonies in November of 1996.

"No man who lived and fought in the battle of Gettysburg did more for his country than Vincent. He was a magnificent soldier, a gentleman of high education and great ability."

General Daniel Butterfield

Completed clay rendering for the statue of Strong Vincent to be displayed in the Erie County Public Library, Erie, Pa. Artist Michael Kraus completed the life size statue in January of 1997.

Notes
&
Bibliography

NOTES

Preface

1. Fox. *Regimental Losses in the American Civil War*, 1888.
2. Howard, W. *Gettysburg Death Roster.* 1990.
3. Chamberlain, Col. J.L. "Through Blood and Fire at Gettysburg." p. 4.

Chapter I

1. Swan, *Harvard Memorial Biographies*, Vol. II, p. 66.
2. Boyd Vincent, *Our Family of Vincents*, p. 104.
3. Ibid., p. 91.
4. Ibid.,
5. Ibid., p. 88.
6. Trinity College Survey to Boyd Vincent, June 1912.
7. Swan, *Biographies*, p. 66.
8. Ibid., pp. 66-67.
9. Johnson, Charles F., "The Journal of Erie Studies." Vol. 17, No. 1, Spring 1988. Erie County Historical Society/ Mercy Heurst College, Erie, PA. pp. 4-6.
    Letter to President E.M. Gallaudet LL.D. from Edger Waterman, Dec. 17, 1912; Gallaudet to Waterman, Dec. 18, 1912, copies in author's possession.
10. Ibid.

11. Swan, *Biographies*, p.67.
12. Harvard Faculty Records XV, May 9, 1857; Jan. 18, 1858; Jan. 17, 1859. Absences From and Tardiness at Recitations and Lectures, 1856-57, 1857-58, 1858-59.

Chapter II

1. Swan, *Biographies*, p. 68.
2. *Erie Weekly Gazette*, May 1, 1861.
3. Norton, *Attack and Defense of Little Round Top*, p. 283.
4. Judson, *History of the Eighty-Third Regiment Pennsylvania Volunteers 1861-1865.* p. 17.

Chapter III

1. Swan, *Biographies*, p. 68.
2. Norton, *ADLRT*, p. 285.
3. Judson, *Eighty-Third*, p. 18.
4. *Proceedings of the Third Brigade Assocation.*
5. Nash, Eugene, *History of the Forty-fourth Regiment*, pp. 45-46.
6. Norton, *ADLRT*, p. 284.
7. Ibid.
8. Ibid.
9. Judson, *Eighty-Third*, p. 22.
10. Judson, *Eighty-Third*, p. 22.

   The following order appears in the Eighty-Third's Orders and Letters Book, 1861 Num. 24:
Headquarters 83rd Reg. Pa. Vols.
December 12th 1861.
Special Order} No. 94

   The men of this command are strictly prohibited until further orders from wearing any portion of the New Zouave Uniform, unless by special permission from these Head Quarters.

Capt. Carpenter will act as Officer of the Day tomorrow.

Lt. White will act as Officer of the Guard.

By order of

Col. Jno. W. McLane.

11. Letter of Miss Sarah Porter, April 2, 1862; copy in author's possession.

12. Letter of Pvt. Daniel B. Foote, 83rd Pa., Feb. 22, 1862. U.S. Army Military History Institute, Carlisle Barracks, PA. Copy in author's possession.

13. Smith, Wayne, "Redemption of the 83rd Pennsylvania." Civil War Magazie, Vol. XXII, p. 38.

Chapter IV

1.   Swan, *Biographies*, p. 69.

2.   Judson, *Eighty-Third*, p. 49.

3.   Ibid, p. 50.

4.   Ibid.

5.   *The Proceedings of the Third Brigade Association*, Sept. 21, 1892, p. 28.

6.   Letter from Miss Sarah Porter, June 14, 1862; copy in author's collection.

7.   Letter from Dr. Brandes, August 7, 1862; copy in author's collection.

8.   Letter from Elizabeth Vincent to Miss Sarah Porter; copy in author's collection.

9.   Letter from Miss Sarah Porter, November 30, 1862; copy in author's collection.

Chapter V

1. Swan, *Biographies*, p. 71.
2. Ibid.
3. Official Records, Vincent's report of Fredericksburg.
4. Judson, *Eighty-Third*, p. 102.
5. Official Records War of the Rebellion, Series I, Vol. XXI
6. Judson, *Eighty-Third*, p. 103.
7. O.R., Series I, Vol. XXI, pp. 412-13.
8. Judson, p. 103.
9. Ibid. p. 104.
10. Ibid. pp. 108-109.
11. O.R. Series I, Vol. XXI, pp. 414.
12. Judson, p. 110.
13. Official Report of General Butterfield.Series I Vol. XXI.

Chapter VI

1. Norton, *ADLRT*, p. 285.
2. Swan, *Biographies*, p. 73.
3. Ibid. p. 72.

Chapter VII

1. Swan, *Biographies*, p. 73.
2. Letter from Vincent to Col. Matthew Quay, April 12, 1863. Regimental letter book. National Archives.
3. O.R. Series I Vol. XXV, p. 171.
4. Judson, *Eighty-Third*, p. 113.
5. Ibid. p. 116.
6. Ibid.

Chapter VIII

1. Judson, *Eighty-Third*, p. 117. See also Chamberlain papers, Library of Congress.
2. Official Records, Series I, Vol. XXVII, p. 614.
3. Robertson, *Michigan in the War*, p. 364-365.
4. Judson, p. 120.
5. O. R., Series I, Vol. XXVII, p. 615.
6. Judson, *Eighty-Third*, p. 121.
7. Ibid. p. 122
8. Boyd Vincent, *Our Family of Vincents*, p. 95.

Chapter IX

1. Norton, Oliver, *The Attack and Defense of Little Round Top.* p. 284.
2. Pfanz, Harry, *Gettysburg the Second Day*, p. 207.
3. Nelson, *Historical Reference book of Erie County.*
4. Gen. G.K. Warren Topographical Map.
5. Norton, *ADLRT*, p. 308. Quoting letter to Farley from Warren.
6. Pfanz, *Gettysburg*, p. 206.
7. Norton, *ADLRT,* p. 263.
8. Ibid. Quoting from Barnes Official Report.
9. Ibid. Sykes Official Report.
10. Warner, *Generals in Blue*, pp. 20-21.
11. Carter, Capt. Robert G., *Four Brothers in Blue*, pp. 259-261.
12. Letter from J.L. Smith to O.W. Norton, Philadelphia, June 1, 1910. Copy in the author's collection.
13. Norton, *Army Letters*, p. 359.
14. Norton, *ADLRT*, p. 264.
15. Ibid.

16. Norton, *Army Letters*, p. 167.
17. Chamberlain, General Joshua Lawrence. "Through Blood and Fire at Gettysburg." p. 4. (It must be noted that Col. Welch states in his official report that the 16th Michigan was at first placed on the left of the 20th Maine before being ordered to the right of the 44th New York just as the attack commenced.)
18. Nash, Eugene, *A History of the Forty-fourth New York Regiment*, p.144.
Judson, *Eighty-Third*, p. 126.
19. Norton, *ADLRT*, p. 171-176.
20. Bennett, Brian A. *A Regimental History of Patrick O'Rorke's 140th Volunteer Infantry*, pp. 210-218.
21. Pfanz, *Gettysburg the Second Day*, p. 228-230.
22. Norton, *Army Letters*, p. 363.
23. Letter from John F. Vincent to D. McConaughy Esq., Nov. 30, 1863; copy in author's collection.
24. Judson, *Eighty-Third*, p. 128.

Chapter X

1. Norton, *ADLRT*, p. 244-245.
2. Judson, *Eighty-Third*, p. 139.
3. Ibid.
4. Ibid.
5. Ibid. p. 140.
6. *Erie Weekly Gazette*, July 16, 1863.
7. Ibid.
8. Ibid.
9. Letter of Miss Sarah Porter, August 16, 1863; copy in author's collection.
10. Letter of Miss Sarah Porter, October 3, 1863; copy in author's collection.
11. Vincent, Our Family of Vincents, p. 103.
12. Speech of O.W. Norton, Little Round Top, Sept. 11, 1889.

BIBLIOGRAPHY

Bates, Samuel P. *History of the Pennsylvania Volunteers, 1861-1865*. 5 vols. Harrisburg: D. Singerly, State Printer, 1869.

Bennett, Brian A. *A Regimental History of Patrick O'Rorke's 140th Volunteer Infantry*. Dayton, Ohio: Morningside. 1992.

Brown, Francis H. *Harvard University in the War of 1861-1865*. Boston: Cupples, Upham and Co., 1886.

Carter, Robert Goldthwaite. *Four Brothers in Blue*. Austin and London, University of Texas Press. 1913.

Chamberlain, Joshua Lawrence. "Through Blood and Fire at Gettysburg." Gettysburg: Stan Clark Military Books, 1994. Reprint of a 1913 article in Hearst's Magazine.

Coco, Gregory A. *A Vast Sea of Misery*. Gettysburg: Thomas Publishing Co., 1988.

Dwight, Benjamin W. *The Descendants of Elder John Strong in America*. 1871. Reprinted by the Strong Family Society of America, 1975.

Fox, William. *Regimental Losses in the American Civil War*. Reprinted by Morningside Books, 1974.

Graham, Ziba B. "On to Gettysburg." A paper read before the Commandery of the State of Michigan. MOLLUS. Detroit: March 2, 1889.

Howard, William. *The Gettysburg Death Roster*, Morningside, 1990.

Judson, Amos M. *History of the 83rd Regiment Pennsylvania Volunteers*. Erie: B.F.H. Lynn Publishers, 1865.

Nash, Eugene A. *A History of the Forty-fourth Regiment, New York Volunteer Infantry in the Civil War*. Chicago: R.R. Donnelly & Sons Company, 1911.

Nelson, S.B. *Historical Reference Book of Erie County*. Erie: S.B. Nelson, 1896.

Norton, Oliver W. *Army Letters, 1861-1865*. Chicago: O.L. Deming, 1903. Reprinted with additional material by Morningside, 1990.

_____. *The Attack and Defense of Little Round Top*. New York: Neale Publishing Company, 1913.

_____. *Strong Vincent and His Brigade at Gettysburg, July 2, 1863*. Chicago, 1909.

Novotny, Debra. "Strong Vincent's Namesake." An article that appeared in the *Battlefield Dispatch*: Newsletter of The Association of Licensed Battlefield Guides, Gettysburg: Sept. 1995.

Pfanz, Harry W. *Gettysburg: The Second Day*. Chapel Hill: University of North Carolina Press, 1987.

Powell, William H. *The Fifth Army Corps*. New York: G.P. Putnam & Sons, 1896.

Proceedings of the Third Brigade Association. New York: Rider and Driver Publishing Co., 1892.

Robertson, Jno. *Michigan in the War*. Lansing: W.S. George & Co., State Printers, 1882.

Sauers, Richard A. *Advance the Colors!* Harrisburg: Capitol Preservation Committee, Commonwealth of Pennsylvania. 1987.

Stafford, David W. *In Defense of the Flag, A True War Story*. Warren, PA.: Warren Mirror Print, 1912.

Swan, William W. *Harvard Memorial Biographies, Vol. II*. Cambridge: Sever and Francis, 1866.

Vincent, Boyd. *Our Family of Vincents*. Cincinnati: Stewart Kidd Company, 1924.

Warner, Ezra J. *Generals in Blue*. Baton Rouge: Louisiana State University Press, 1964.

INDEX

Photo Credits

Page 10, Erie County Historical Society; pages 12 & 13 taken from *Our Family of Vincent's*; page 19, Erie County Historical Society; page 20, The Harvard University Archives; page 24, Ronn Palm; page 25, Miss Porter's School, Farmington, CT.; page 52, Ronn Palm; page 56, Pennsylvania Historical Commission; pages 66 & 78, MOLLUS Collection, U.S. Army Military History Institute Carlisle Barracks, PA.; pages 89 & 90, William B. Styple; page 91, MOLLUS Collection, Craig Caba; page 92, Christine L. Wolfe; pages 96, 98,& 114, Myra & Jim Wright; page 116, (top) William B. Styple, (bottom) Gettysburg National Military Park; page 122, James H. Nevins; page 127, Peter Hakel; page 146, Ronn Palm; page 160, Mike Kraus.

About the Authors

James H. Nevins is a veteran of the Army Military Intelligence Branch, and a graduate of New Jersey's Upsala College. In an another life he is a police sergeant in Elizabeth, New Jersey.

William B. Styple is a graduate of Catawba College and operates a business in his native Kearny, New Jersey, where he is also Town Historian. He is currently writing a biography on the life of General Philip Kearny.